North Carolina Convention

Ordinances and Resolutions Passed by the State Convention of North Carolina

North Carolina Convention

Ordinances and Resolutions Passed by the State Convention of North Carolina

ISBN/EAN: 9783337812393

Printed in Europe, USA, Canada, Australia, Japan

Cover: Foto ©Suzi / pixelio.de

More available books at **www.hansebooks.com**

ORDINANCES AND RESOLUTIONS

PASSED BY

THE STATE CONVENTION

OF

NORTH CAROLINA.

.

𝔉irst 𝔖ession in 𝔐ay and 𝔍une, 1861.

———————

RALEIGH:

JOHN W. SYME, PRINTER TO THE CONVENTION.

1862.

ORDINANCES AND RESOLUTIONS

OF THE

STATE CONVENTION

OF

NORTH CAROLINA.

FIRST SESSION IN MAY AND JUNE, 1861.

AN ORDINANCE TO DISSOLVE THE UNION BE- [No. 1.]
TWEEN THE STATE OF NORTH CAROLINA
AND THE OTHER STATES UNITED WITH HER
UNDER THE COMPACT OF GOVERNMENT
ENTITLED THE CONSTITUTION OF THE
UNITED STATES.

We, the people of the State of North Carolina, in Convention assembled, do declare and ordain, and it is hereby declared and ordained, That the ordinance adopted by the State of North Carolina in the Convention of 1789, whereby the Constitution of the United States was ratified and adopted, and also, all acts and parts of acts of the General Assembly, ratifying and adopting amendments to the said Constitution, are hereby repealed, rescinded and abrogated. [Repeals Ordinance ratifying Constitution of the United States]

We do further declare and ordain, That the union now subsisting between the State of North Carolina and the other States under the title of the United States of America, is hereby dissolved, and that the State of North Carolina is in the full possession and exercise of all those rights of sovereignty which belong and appertain to a free and independent State. [*Ratified the 20th day of May,* 1861.] [Declares the Union of N. C. with the U. S. dissolved.]

[No. 2.] AN ORDINANCE VESTING IN THE CONFEDER-
ATE STATES OF AMERICA JURISDICTION
OVER CERTAIN TRACTS OF LAND IN THE
TOWN OF FAYETTEVILLE, N. C.

*We, the people of North Carolina, in Convention assem-
bled, do declare and ordain, and it is hereby declared and
ordained,* That the jurisdiction of the State of North Carolina is hereby ceded to the Confederate States of America,
for the purpose of maintaining and erecting therein Arsenals, Magazines, or other necessary buildings, over all
that tract, piece or parcel of land, situate, lying and being
in the town of Fayetteville and county of Cumberland, the
jurisdiction over which was ceded the United States of
America by an act of the General Assembly of the State
of North Carolina, ratified on the 8th day of January,
1838, and is entitled "An Act vesting in the United
States of America jurisdiction over a certain tract of land
in the town of Fayetteville and county of Cumberland."

And be it further declared and ordained, That jurisdiction in like manner and for like purposes is hereby ceded
to the Confederate States of America over all tracts or
parcels of land adjacent to the same heretofore purchased
by the United States of America.

And be it further declared and ordained, That the jurisdiction so ceded to the Confederate States of America, is
granted upon the express condition that the State of North
Carolina shall retain jurisdiction on and over the tracts of
land aforesaid, so far that civil process in all cases, and
such criminal process as may issue under the authority of
the State of North Carolina, against any person or persons charged with crimes committed without said tract of
land may be executed therein in the same way and manner
as if this jurisdiction had not yet been ceded: The Confederate States to retain the said jurisdiction so long as
said tract or tracts of land shall be used for the purposes
expressed in this ordinance, and no longer.

Be it further ordained, That the title and possession of
the said lands is hereby ceded to the said Confederate
States on the terms and conditions aforesaid. [*Ratified
the 5th day of June, 1861.*]

AN ORDINANCE TO PROVIDE FOR THE AP- [No. 3.] PIONTMENT OF A BOARD OF CLAIMS.

Be it ordained, &c., That a Board of Claims, to consist Number of members and of three members—two of whom shall be a quorum to do duties. business—be elected by this Convention, whose duty it shall be to audit and settle, upon principles of equity and justice, all claims that may be presented against the State for expenses incurred towards the arming, equipping, sub- sistence and transportation of our volunteer troops, and of munitions of war, and for bounty paid said troops either in the military or naval service of the State, and other ex- penses incurred in the defence of the State prior to the 20th of May, 1861; and all county claims and other claims of the character aforesaid, arising since the 20th of May, 1861, which are not provided for by law; and no county or corporation claim shall be entertained by said Board, unless the same shall be certified by the County Trustee, or Chairman of the County Court, or by the corporate authorities of any corporation, as the case may be, whence the claim or claims may come.

Be it further ordained. That the members of the said To take an oath. Board of Claims shall take and subscribe an oath faithfully and impartially to discharge their duties; they may em- Employ a Clerk. ploy a clerk who shall record the proceedings of the Board; they shall give general and public notice of the times and place of their sittings; they shall be authorized to admin- ister oaths and to require affidavits to be made when neces- sary. The said Board shall report the result of their labors To report to the Convention. and proceedings, with a brief statement of the character of each claim allowed, at the conclusion of their labors, or from time to time, as they may think proper, to this Con- vention, either at the present or any future session. Each Compensation. member of the Board shall be allowed six dollars per day, and the clerk shall be allowed four dollars per day for each day they shall be actually employed.

Be it further ordained, That this ordinance shall re- Length of time the Board shall main in force, and the Board hereby provided for shall con- exist. tinue in existence till the 15th day of December next, subject to amendment, modification or repeal by this Convention; and, in case of the death, resignation or refusal to serve of any member of said Board of Claims during any recess, or after the final adjournment of this Convention, such vacancy shall be supplied by the appointment of the Governor. [*Ratified the 8th day of June*, 1861.]

[No. 4] AN ORDINANCE TOUCHING THE AUTHENTICATION OF ORDINANCES AND OTHER ACTS OF THE CONVENTION.

Be it ordained by this Convention, That ordinances and resolutions of this Convention having the effect of laws, shall be authenticated by the signature of the President and attestation of the Secretary and Assistant Secretary, and shall have the date of their final passage annexed thereto; from which date each ordinance and resolution shall take effect and go into operation, unless some other time shall be therein appointed. [*Ratified the 8th day of June*, 1861.]

[No. 5.] RESOLUTION IN FAVOR OF L. W. JOYNER.

Resolved, That the Treasurer be, and he is hereby authorized to pay L. W. Joyner, sixty-eight dollars for services as clerk of the Military Committee. [*Ratified the 15th day of June*, 1861.]

[No. 6.] RESOLUTION TO AUTHORIZE THE FIRST REGIMENT TO INSCRIBE "BETHEL" ON THEIR COLORS.

Resolved, That this Convention, appreciating the valor and good conduct of the officers and men in the 1st Regiment of North Carolina Volunteers, do, as a testimonial of the same, authorize the said regiment to inscribe the word "Bethel" upon their regimental colors. [*Ratified the 17th day of June*, 1861.]

AN ORDINANCE DEFINING TREASON AGAINST [No. 7.] THE STATE.

Be it ordained by this Convention, and it is hereby Consists in levy-
ordained by the authority of the same, as follows: Treason
against the State of North Carolina, shall consist only in
levying war against her, or in adhering to her enemies,
giving them aid and comfort.   No person shall be convicted Two witnesses
of Treason unless on the testimony of two witnesses to the to convict.
same overt act, or confession in open court. [*Ratified the*
18*th day of June*, 1861.]

AN ORDINANCE REPEALING THE ACT OF THE [No. 8.] GENERAL ASSEMBLY CONVENING THE LEG-ISLATURE ON THE 25TH OF JUNE, 1861.

Be it ordained, That the resolution passed by the Gen- Abrogates reso-
eral Assembly at its late session providing for an adjourned lature.
session of the said General Assembly on the 25th of June,
1861, be, and the same is hereby abrogated and annulled.
 Be it further ordained, That there shall be a session of Appoints a day.
the General Assembly which shall convene on the 15th day
of August next. [*Ratified the* 19*th day of June*, 1861.]

RESOLUTIONS FIXING THE COMPENSATION [No. 9.] OF OFFICERS OF THE CONVENTION, AND APPOINTING AN AUDITING COMMITTEE.

Resolved, That the President, Secretaries, Engrossing Salaries to be
Clerk and Doorkeepers of this Convention be allowed the lowed by the
same compensation which is paid by the General Assembly bly.
to the officers who render similar services to that body.
 Resolved, That a committee of three be appointed, who Contingent ex-
shall, during the sitting or after the adjournment of the penses.
Convention, audit and certify to the Governor all other

claims on account of the contingent expenses of the Convention, and that they be authorized to allow three dollars per day and the travelling expenses of all messengers who may be employed by this Convention. [*Ratified the* 19*th day of June*, 1861.]

[No. 10.] RESOLUTION TO PRINT ARMY REGULATIONS.

Resolved, That four thousand copies of the Army Regulations of the Army of the Confederate States of America be printed for the use of the officers and soldiers of this State, now in service, and hereafter to be called into service.

Resolved, That ten copies each be furnished to the members of this Convention, and that the Adjutant General be requested to distribute the remainder in such manner as to furnish to our soldiers a knowledge of the military laws by which they are to be governed. [*Ratified the* 19*th day of June*, 1861.]

[No. 11.] AN ORDINANCE TO RATIFY THE CONSTITUTION OF THE CONFEDERATE STATES OF AMERICA.

WHEREAS, On the eleventh day of March, A. D., 1861, at Montgomery, in the State of Alabama, a Constitution was adopted by a Congress of delegates from the States of Alabama, Florida, Georgia, Louisiana, Mississippi, South Carolina and Texas, united under the name of the Confederate States of America, which Constitution hath been ratified by each of the said States:

Now, therefore, this Convention, having seen and considered the said Constitution, doth, in behalf of the people of the State of North Carolina, adopt and ratify the said Constitution and form of Government, the tenor of which appears in a schedule hereto annexed.

CONSTITUTION OF THE CONFEDERATE STATES OF AMERICA.

We, the people of the Confederate States, each State *Preamble* acting in its sovereign and independent character, in order to form a permanent federal government, establish justice, insure domestic tranquility and secure the blessings of lib erty to ourselves and our posterity—invoking the favor and guidance of Almighty God—do ordain and establish this Constitution for the Confederate States of America.

ARTICLE 1.

SECTION I.

All legislative powers herein delegated shall be vested *Vests the Legislative powers* in a Congress of the Confederate States, which shall consist of a Senate and House of Representatives.

SECTION II.

1. The House of Representatives shall be composed of *Qualifications of Electors.* members chosen every second year by the people of the several States; and the electors in each State shall be citizens of the Confederate States, and have the qualifications requisite for electors of the most numerous branch of the State Legislature; but no person of foreign birth, not a citizen of the Confederate States, shall be allowed to vote for any officer, civil or political, State or Federal.

2. No person shall be a Representative, who shall not *Qualifications of Representatives* have attained the age of twenty-five years, and be a citizen of the Confederate States, and who shall not, when elected, be an inhabitant of that State in which he shall be chosen.

3. Representatives and Direct Taxes shall be appor- *Apportionment* tioned among the several States, which may be included within this Confederacy, according to their respective numbers, which shall be determined, by adding to the whole number of free persons, including those bound to service

2

for a term of years, and excluding Indians not taxed, three-fifths of all slaves. The actual enumeration shall be made within three years after the first meeting of the Congress of the Confederate States, and within every subsequent term of ten years, in such manner as they shall by law direct. The number of Representatives shall not exceed one for every fifty thousand, but each State shall have at least one Representative; and until such enumeration shall be made, the State of South Carolina shall be entitled to choose six—the State of Georgia ten—the State of Alabama nine—the State of Florida two—the State of Mississippi seven—the State of Louisiana six, and the State of Texas six.

4. When vacancies happen in the representation from any State, the Executive authority thereof shall issue writs of election to fill such vacancies.

5. The House of Representatives shall choose their Speaker and other officers; and shall have the sole power of impeachment: except that any judicial or other federal officer, resident and acting solely within the limits of any State, may be impeached by a vote of two-thirds of both branches of the Legislature thereof.

SECTION III.

1. The Senate of the Confederate States shall be composed of two Senators from each State, chosen for six years by the Legislature thereof, at the regular session next immediately preceding the commencement of the term of service: and each Senator shall have one vote.

2. Immediately after they shall be assembled, in consequence of the first election, they shall be divided as equally as may be into three classes. The seats of the Senators of the first class shall be vacated at the expiration of the second year; of the second class at the expiration of the fourth year; and of the third class at the expiration of the sixth year; so that one-third may be chosen every second year; and if vacancies happen by resignation, or oth-

erwise, during the recess of the Legislature of any State, the executive thereof may make temporary appointments until the meeting of the Legislature, which shall then fill such vacancies.

3. No person shall be a Senator who shall not have at- *Qualifications of Senators.* tained the age of thirty years, and be a citizen of the Confederate States, and who shall not, when elected, be an inhabitant of the State for which he shall be chosen.

4. The Vice-President of the Confederate States shall *Vice President* be President of the Senate, but shall have no vote, unless they be equally divided.

5. The Senate shall choose their other officers ; and also *Other officers of Senate.* a President *pro tempore* in the absence of the Vice-President, or when he shall exercise the office of President of the Confederate States.

6. The Senate shall have the sole power to try all im- *Powers of Senate.* peachments. When sitting for that purpose, they shall be on oath or affirmation. When the President of the Confederate States is tried, the Chief Justice shall preside ; and no person shall be convicted without the concurrence of two-thirds of the members present.

7. Judgment in cases of impeachment shall not extend *Extent of judgment.* further than to removal from office, and disqualification to hold and enjoy any office of honor, trust or profit, under the Confederate States; but the party convicted shall, nevertheless, be liable and subject to indictment, trial, judgment and punishment according to law.

SECTION IV.

1. The times, places and manner of holding elections *Times and manner of holding elections.* for Senators and Representatives, shall be prescribed in each State by the Legislature thereof, subject to the provisions of this constitution ; but the Congress may, at any time, by law, make or alter such regulations, except as to the times and places of choosing Senators.

2. The Congress shall assemble at least once in every *Congress to meet once every year.* year ; and such meeting shall be on the first Monday in December, unless they shall, by law, appoint a different day.

SECTION V.

1. Each House shall be the judge of the elections, returns and qualifications of its own members, and a majority of each shall constitute a quorum to do business; but a smaller number may adjourn from day to day, and may be authorized to compel the attendance of absent members, in such manner and under such penalties as each House may provide.

2. Each House may determine the rules of its proceedings, punish its members for disorderly behavior, and, with the concurrence of two-thirds of the whole number, expel a member.

3. Each House shall keep a journal of its proceedings, and from time to time, publish the same, excepting such parts as may in their judgment require secrecy; and the yeas and nays of the members of either House, on any question, shall, at the desire of one-fifth of those present, be entered on the journal.

4. Neither House, during the session of Congress, shall, without the consent of the other, adjourn for more than three days, nor to any other place than that in which the two Houses shall be sitting.

SECTION VI.

1. The Senators and Representatives shall receive a compensation for their services, to be ascertained by law, and paid out of the treasury of the Confederate States.— They shall, in all cases, except treason, felony and breach of the peace, be privileged from arrest during their attendance at the session of their respective houses, and in going to and returning from the same; and for any speech or debate in either house, they shall not be questioned in any other place.

2. No Senator or Representative shall, during the time for which he was elected, be appointed to any civil office under the authority of the Confederate States, which shall

have been created, or the emoluments whereof shall have
been increased during such time; and no person holding
any office under the Confederate States shall be a member
of either· house during his continuance in office. But Congress may, by law, grant to the principal officer in each
of the Executive Departments a seat upon the floor of
either house, with the privilege of discussing any measures
appertaining to his department.

SECTION VII.

1. All bills for raising revenue shall originate in the Bills for raising
House of Representative; but the Senate may propose or Revenue.
concur with amendments as on other bills.

2. Every bill which shall have passed both houses, shall, Bills to be sign-
before it becomes a law, be presented to the President of dent.
the Confederate States; if he approve, he shall sign it;
but if not, he shall return it with his objections to that
house in which it shall have originated, who shall enter the
objections at large on their journal, and proceed to recon-
sider it. If, after such reconsideration, two-thirds of that
house shall agree to pass the bill, it shall be sent, together
with the objections, to the other house, by which it shall
likewise be reconsidered, and if approved by two-thirds of
that house, it shall become a law. But in all such cases,
the votes of both houses shall be determined by yeas and
nays, and the names of the persons voting for and against
the bill shall be entered on the journal of each house respectively. If any bill shall not be returned by the President within ten days (Sundays excepted) after it shall have
been presented to him, the same shall be a law, in like
manner as if he had signed it, unless the Congress, by their
adjournment, prevent its return; in which case it shall not
be a law. The President may approve any appropriation
and disapprove any other appropriation in the same bill
In such case he shall, in signing the bill, designate the appropriations disapproved; and shall return a copy of such
appropriations, with his objections, to the house in which

the bill shall have originated; and the same proceedings shall then be had as in the case of other bills disapproved by the President.

3. Every order, resolution or vote, to which the concurrence of both houses may be necessary, (except on a question of adjournment) shall be presented to the President of the Confederate States: and before the same shall take effect, shall be approved by him; or being disapproved by him, shall be repassed by two-thirds of both houses, according to the rules and limitations prescribed in the case of a bill.

SECTION VIII.

The Congress shall have power:

1. To lay and collect taxes, duties, imposts and excises, for revenue necessary to pay the debts, provide for the common defence, and carry on the government of the Confederate States: but no bounties shall be granted from the treasury; nor shall any duties or taxes on importations from foreign nations be laid to promote or foster any branch of industry; and all duties, imposts, and excises shall be uniform throughout the Confederate States:

2. To borrow money on the credit of the Confederate States:

3. To regulate commerce with foreign nations, and among the several States, and with the Indian tribes; but neither this, nor any other clause contained in the constitution, shall ever be construed to delegate the power to Congress to appropriate money for any internal improvement intended to facilitate commerce; except for the purpose of furnishing lights, beacons, and buoys, and other aids to navigation upon the coasts, and improvement of harbors and the removing of obstructions in river navigation, in all which cases, such duties shall be laid on the navigation facilitated thereby, as may be necessary to pay the costs and expenses thereof:

4. To establish uniform laws of naturalization, and uni- Laws of naturalization..
form laws on the subject of bankruptcies, throughout the
Confederate States, but no law of Congress shall discharge
any debt contracted before the passage of the same:

5. To coin money, regulate the value thereof and of Coining money.
foreign coin, and fix the standard of weights and measures:

6. To provide for the punishment of counterfeiting the Punishment for counterfeiting.
securities and current coin of the Confederate States:

7. To establish postoffices and post routes; but the ex- Post Offices and post routes.
penses of the Postoffice Department, after the first day of
March in the year of our Lord eighteen hundred and sixty-three, shall be paid out of its own revenues:

8. To promote the progress of science and useful arts, Science and useful arts.
by securing for limited times to authors and inventors the
exclusive right to their respective writings and discoveries:

9. To constitute tribunals inferior to the Supreme Inferior tribunals.
Court:

10. To define and punish piracies and felonies committed Piracies and felonies.
on the high seas, and offences against the law of nations:

11. To declare war, grant letters of marque and repri- To declare war.
sal, and make rules concerning captures on land and water:

12. To raise and support armies; but no appropriation Armies.
of money to that use shall be for a longer term than two
years:

13. To provide and maintain a navy: Navy.

14. To make rules for the government and regulation of Rules for Army and Navy
the land and naval forces:

15. To provide for calling forth the militia to execute The militia.
the laws of the Confederate States, suppress insurrections,
and repel invasions:

16. To provide for organizing, arming and disciplining Organizing, arming, &c.
the militia, and for governing such part of them as may
be employed in the service of the Confederate States;
reserving to the States, respectively, the appointment of
the officers, and the authority of training the militia
according to the discipline prescribed by Congress.

17. To exercise exclusive legislation, in all cases what- Seat of Government.
soever, over such district (not exceeding ten miles square)

as may, by cession of one or more States and the acceptance of Congress, become the seat of the Government of the Confederate States; and to exercise like authority over all purchased by the consent of the legislature of the State in which the same shall be, for the erection of forts, magazines, arsenals, dockyards and other needful buildings; and

18. To make all laws which shall be necessary and proper for carrying into execution the foregoing powers, and all other powers vested by this Constitution in the government of the Confederate States, or in any department or officer thereof.

SECTION IX.

1. The importation of negroes of the African race, from any foreign country, other than the slaveholding States or territories of the United States of America, is hereby forbidden; and Congress is required to pass such laws as shall effectually prevent the same.

2. Congress shall also have power to prohibit the introduction of slaves from any State not a member of, or territory not belonging to this Confederacy.

3. The privilege of the writ of habeas corpus shall not be suspended, unless when in cases of rebellion or invasion the public safety may require it.

4. No bill of attainder, *ex post facto* law, or law denying or impairing the right of property in negro slaves shall be passed.

5. No capitation or other direct tax shall be laid, unless in proportion to the census or enumeration hereinbefore directed to be taken.

6. No tax or duty shall be laid on articles exported from any State, except by a vote of two-thirds of both houses.

7. No preference shall be given by any regulation of commerce or revenue to the ports of one State over those of another.

8. No money shall be drawn from the treasury, but in consequence of appropriations made by law ; and a regular statement and account of the receipts and expenditures of all public money shall be published from time to time. Money drawn from the Treasury.

9. Congress shall appropriate no money from the treasury except by a vote of two-thirds of both houses, taken by yeas and nays, unless it be asked and estimated for by some one of the heads of department, and submitted to Congress by the President : or for the purpose of paying its own expenses and contingences ; or for the payment of claims against the Confederate States, the justice of which shall have been judicially declared by a tribunal for the investigation of claims against the government, which it is hereby made the duty of Congress to establish. Appropriations.

10. All bills appropriating money shall specify in federal currency the exact amount of each appropriation and the purposes for which it is made : and Congress shall grant no extra compensation to any public contractor, officer, agent or servant, after such contract shall have been made or such service rendered. Amount appropriated to be specified on bills

11. No title of nobility shall be granted by the Confederate States ; and no person holding any office of profit or trust under them, shall, without the consent of the Congress, accept of any present, emolument, office or title of any kind whatever from any king, prince or foreign State. Presents from foreign potentates.

12. Congress shall make no law respecting an establishment of religion, or prohibiting the free exercise thereof ; or abridging the freedom of speech, or of the press : or the right of the people peaceably to assemble and petition the government for a redress of grievances. Religion, freedom of speech and right of petition.

13. A well regulated militia being necessary to the security of a free State, the right of the people to keep and bear arms shall not be infringed. Arms-bearing.

14. No soldier shall, in time of peace, be quartered in any house without the consent of the owner ; nor in time of war, but in a manner to be prescribed by law. Soldiers and house owners

15. The right of the people to be secure in their persons, houses, papers, and effects against unreasonable Searches.

3

searches and seizures, shall not be violated; and no warrants shall issue but upon probable cause, supported by oath or affirmation, and particularly describing the place to be searched, and the persons or thing to be seized.

16. No person shall be held to answer for a capital or otherwise infamous crime, unless on a presentment or indictment of a grand jury, except in cases arising in the land or naval forces, or in the militia, when in actual service, in time of war or public danger; nor shall any person be subject for the same offence to be twice put in jeopardy of life or limb; nor to be compelled, in any criminal case, to be a witness against himself; nor be deprived of life, liberty, or property without due process of law; nor shall private property be taken for public use without just compensation.

17. In all criminal prosecutions the accused shall enjoy the right to a speedy and public trial, by an impartial jury of the State and district wherein the crime shall have been committed, which district shall have been previously ascertained by law, and to be informed of the nature and cause of the accusation; to be confronted with the witnesses against him; to have compulsory process for obtaining witnesses in his favor; and to have the assistance of counsel for his defence.

18. In suits at common law, where the value in controversy shall exceed twenty dollars, the right of trial by jury shall be preserved; and no fact so tried by a jury shall be otherwise re-examined in any court of the Confederacy, than according to the rules of the common law.

19. Excessive bail shall not be required, nor excessive fines imposed, nor cruel and unusual punishments inflicted.

20. Every law or resolution having the force of law, shall relate but to one subject, and that shall be expressed in the title.

SECTION X.

1. No State shall enter into any treaty, alliance, or confederation; grant letters of marque and reprisal; coin

money; make anything but gold and silver coin a tender
in payment of debts ; pass any bill of attainder, or *ex post
facto* law, or law impairing the obligation of contracts; or
grant any title of nobility.

2. No State shall, without the consent of the Congress, Prohibition upon States.
lay any imposts or duties on imports or exports, except
what may be absolutely necessary for executing its inspection laws; and the net produce of all duties and imposts,
laid by any State on imports or exports, shall be for the
use of the treasury of the Confederate States ; and all
such laws shall be subject to the revision and control of
Congress.

3. No State shall, without the consent of Congress, lay
any duty on tonnage, except on sea-going vessels, for the
improvement of its rivers and harbors navigated by the
said vessels; but such duties shall not conflict with any
treaties of the Confederate States with foreign nations:
and any surplus revenue, thus derived, after making such
improvement, be paid into the common treasury. Nor
shall any State keep troops or ships of war in time of peace,
enter into any agreement or compact with another State,
or with a foreign power, or engage in war, unless actually
invaded, or in such imminent danger as will not admit of
delay.   But when any river divides or flows through two or
more States, they may enter into compacts with each other
to improve the navigation thereof.

ARTICLE 2.

SECTION 1.

1. The executive power shall be vested in a President of President and Vice President.
the Confederate States of America. He and the Vice
President shall hold their offices for the term of six years;
but the President shall not be re-eligible. The President
and Vice President shall be elected as follows :

2. Each State shall appoint, in such manner as the leg- Electors.
islature thereof may direct, a number of electors equal to

the whole number of Senators and Representatives to which the State may be entitled in the Congress; but no Senator or Representative, or person holding an office of trust or profit under the Confederate States, shall be appointed an elector.

Balloting for President and Vice President

3. The electors shall meet in their respective States and vote by ballot for President and Vice President, one of whom, at least, shall not be an inhabitant of the same State with themselves; they shall name in their ballots the person voted for as President, and in distinct ballots the person voted for as Vice President, and they shall make distinct lists of all persons voted for as President, and of all persons voted for as Vice President, and of the number of votes for each, which lists they shall sign and certify, and transmit, sealed, to the seat of the government of the Confederate States, directed to the President of the Senate:

Counting the vote

the President of the Senate shall, in the presence of the Senate and House of Representatives, open all the certificates, and the votes shall then be counted: the person having the greatest number of votes for President shall be the President, if such a number be a majority of the whole number of electors appointed; and if no person have such majority, then, from the persons having the highest numbers, not exceeding three, on the list of those voted for as President, the House of Representatives shall choose,

Manner of choosing the President by the House of Representatives

immediately, by ballot, the President. But in choosing the President, the votes shall be taken by States, the representation from each State having one vote; a quorum for this purpose shall consist of a member or members from two-thirds of the States, and a majority of all the States shall be necessary to a choice. And if the House of Representatives shall not choose a President, whenever the right of choice shall devolve upon them, before the fourth day of March next following, then the Vice-President shall act as President, as in case of the death, or other constitutional disability of the President.

Vice President.

4. The person having the greatest number of votes as Vice-President, shall be the Vice-President, if such num-

ber be a majority of the whole number of electors
appointed; and if no person have a majority, then, from
the two highest numbers on the list the Senate shall choose
the Vice-President; a quorum for the purpose shall consist of two-thirds of the whole number of Senators, and a
majority of the whole number shall be necessary to a
choice.

5. But no person constitutionally ineligible to the office Eligibility.
of President shall be eligible to that of Vice-President of
the Confederate States.

6. The Congress may determine the time of choosing Time of choos-
the electors, and the day on which they shall give their ing electors.
votes: which day shall be the same throughout the Confederate States.

7. No person, except a natural born citizen of the Con- Qualifications of
federate States, or a citizen thereof at the time of the President.
adoption of this Constitution, or a citizen thereof, born in
the United States prior to the 20th of December, 1860,
shall be eligible to the office of President; neither shall
any person be eligible to that office who shall not have
attained the age of thirty-five years, and been fourteen
years a resident within the limits of the Confederate States,
as they may exist at the time of his election.

8. In case of the removal of the President from office, Removal, death,
or of his death, resignation, or inability to discharge the ident.
powers and duties of the said office, the same shall devolve &c., of the Pres-
on the Vice-President; and the Congress may, by law,
provide for the case of removal, death, resignation, or
inability both of the President and Vice-President, declaring what officer shall then act as President, and such officer
shall act accordingly until the disability be removed or a
President shall be elected.

9. The President shall, at stated times, receive for his Compensation.
services a compensation, which shall neither be increased
nor diminished during the period for which he shall have
been elected; and he shall not receive within that period
any other emolument from the Confederate States, or any
of them.

10. Before he enters on the execution of his office, he
shall take the following oath or affirmation :

"I do solemnly swear (or affirm) that I will faithfully
execute the office of the President of the Confederate
States, and will to the best of my ability, preserve, protect,
and defend the Constitution thereof."

SECTION II.

1. The President shall be commander-in-chief of the
army and navy of the Confederate States, and of the
militia of the several States, when called into the actual
service of the Confederate States ; he may require the
opinion, in writing, of the principal officer in each of the
Executive Departments, upon any subject relating to the
duties of their respective offices ; and he shall have power
to grant reprieves and pardons for offences against the
Confederate States, except in cases of impeachment.

2. He shall have power, by and with the advice and
consent of the Senate, to make treaties, provided two-
thirds of the Senators present concur ; and he shall nomi-
nate, and by and with the advice and consent of the Senate, shall appoint ambassadors, other public ministers and
consuls, Judges of the Supreme Court, and all other
officers of the Confederate States, whose appointments are
not herein otherwise provided for, and which shall be
established by law ; but the Congress may, by law, vest the
appointment of such inferior officers, as they think proper,
in the President alone, in the courts of law or in the heads
of Departments.

3. The principal officer in each of the Executive Departments, and all persons connected with the diplomatic service, may be removed from office at the pleasure of the
President. All other civil officers of the Executive Department may be removed at any time by the President, or
other appointing power, when their services are unneces-
sary, or for dishonesty, incapacity, inefficiency, misconduct,
or neglect of duty ; and when so removed, the removal

shall be reported to the Senate, together with the reasons therefor.

4. The President shall have power to fill all vacancies *Vacancies.* that may happen during the recess of the Senate, by granting commissions which shall expire at the end of their next session; but no person rejected by the Senate shall be re-appointed to the same office during their ensuing recess.

SECTION III.

1. The President shall, from time to time, give to the *Duties of President.* Congress information of the state of the Confederacy, and recommend to their consideration such measures as he shall judge necessary and expedient; he may, on extraordinary occasions, convene both houses, or either of them ; and in case of disagreement between them, with respect to the time of adjournment, he may adjourn them to such time as he shall think proper ; he shall receive ambassadors and other public ministers; he shall take care that the laws be faithfully executed, and shall commission all the officers of the Confederate States.

SECTION IV.

1. The President, Vice-President, and all civil officers *Punishment of high officers for for treason, bribery, &c.* of the Confederate States, shall be removed from office on impeachment for, and conviction of, treason, bribery, or other high crimes and misdemeanors.

ARTICLE III.

SECTION I.

1. The judicial power of the Confederate States shall be *The Judiciary* vested in one Supreme Court, and in such Inferior Courts as the Congress may from time to time ordain and establish. The judges, both of the Supreme and Inferior Courts, shall hold their offices during good behavior, and shall, at

stated times, receive for their services a compensation, which shall not be diminished during their continuance in office.

SECTION II.

1. The judicial power shall extend to all cases arising under this Constitution, the laws of the Confederate States, and treaties made or which shall be made under their authority; to all cases affecting ambassadors, other public ministers and consuls; to all cases of admiralty and maritime jurisdiction; to controversies to which the Confederate States shall be a party; to controversies between two or more States; between a State and citizen of another State where the State is plaintiff; between citizens claiming lands under grants of different States; and between a State or the citizens thereof, and foreign States, citizens or subjects: but no State shall be sued by a citizen or subject of any foreign State.

2. In all cases affecting ambassadors, other public ministers, and consuls, and those in which a State shall be a party, the Supreme Court shall have original jurisdiction. In all the other cases before mentioned, the Supreme Court shall have appellate jurisdiction, both as to law and fact, with such exceptions, and under such regulations as the Congress shall make.

3. The trial of all crimes, except in cases of impeachment, shall be by jury, and such trial shall be held in the State where the said crimes shall have been committed; but when not committed within any State, the trial shall be at such place or places as the Congress may by law have directed.

SECTION III.

1. Treason against the Confederate States shall consist only in levying war against them, or in adhering to their enemies, giving them aid and comfort. No person shall be convicted of treason unless on the testimony of two witnesses to the same overt act or on confession in open court.

2. The Congress shall have power to declare the punish- Punishment. ment of treason, but no attainder of treason shall work corruption of blood, or forfeiture, except during the life of the person attainted.

ARTICLE IV.

SECTION I.

1. Full faith and credit shall be given in each State to State relations. the public acts, records and judicial proceedings of every other State. And the Congress may, by general laws, prescribe the manner in which such acts, records and proceedings shall be proved, and the effect thereof.

SECTION II.

1. The citizens of each State shall be entitled to all the Rights of citizens. privileges and immunities of citizens in the several States, and shall have the right of transit and sojourn in any State of this Confederacy, with their slaves and other property; and the right of property in said slaves shall not be thereby impaired.

2. A person charged in any State with treason, felony, Criminals. or other crime against the laws of such a State, who shall flee from justice, and be found in another State, shall, on demand of the Executive authority of the State from which he fled, be delivered up, to be removed to the State having jurisdiction of the crime.

3. No slave or other person held to service or labor in Fugitives from labor. any State or territory of the Confederate States under the laws thereof, escaping or lawfully carried into another, shall, in consequence of any law or regulation therein, be discharged from such service or labor; but shall be delivered up on claim of the party to whom such slave belongs, or to whom such service or labor may be due.

4

SECTION III.

Admission of new States

1. Other States may be admitted into this Confederacy by a vote of two-thirds of the whole House of Representatives, and two-thirds of the Senate, the Senate voting by States; but no new State shall be formed or erected within the jurisdiction of any other State; nor any State be formed by the junction of two or more States, or parts of States, without the consent of the Legislatures of the States concerned as well as of the Congress.

Power of Congress

2. The Congress shall have power to dispose of and make all needful rules and regulations concerning the property of the Confederate States, including the lands thereof.

Acquisition of new territory

3. The Confederate States may acquire new territory; and Congress shall have power to legislate and provide governments for the inhabitants of all territory belonging to the Confederate States, lying without the limits of the several States; and may permit them, at such times, and in such manner as it may by law provide, to form States to be admitted into the Confederacy. In all such territory, the institution of negro slavery as it now exists in the Confederate States, shall be recognized and protected by Congress, and by the territorial government; and the inhabitants of the several Confederate States and territories, shall have the right to take to such territory any slaves lawfully held by them in any of the States or territories of the Confederate States.

Each of the several States are to be guarantied

4. The Confederate States shall guaranty to every State that now is or hereafter may become a member of this Confederacy, a Republican form of government, and shall protect each of them against invasion; and on application of the Legislature (or of the Executive when the Legislature is not in session) against domestic violence.

ARTICLE V.

SECTION I.

Convention of all the States

1. Upon the demand of any three States, legally assembled in their several conventions, the Congress shall sum-

mon a convention of all the States, to take into consideration such amendments to the Constitution as the said States
shall concur in suggesting at the time when the said
demand is made; and should any of the proposed amendments to the Constitution be agreed on by the said convention—voting by States—and the same be ratified by the
legislatures of two-thirds of the several States, or by conventions in two-thirds thereof—as the one or the other
mode of ratification may be proposed by the general convention—they shall from thenceforward form a part of this
constitution. But no State shall, without its consent, be
deprived of its equal representation in the Senate.

ARTICLE VI.

1. The Government established by this Constitution is *The Permanent and the Provisional Government.*
the successor of the Provisional Government of the Con-
federate States of America, and all the laws passed by the
latter shall continue in force until the same shall be repealed or modified; and all the officers appointed by the
same shall remain in office until their successors are appointed and qualified, or the offices abolished.

2. All debts contracted and engagements entered into *Debts.*
before the adoption of this Constitution shall be as valid
against the Confederate States under this Constitution as
under the Provisional Government.

3. This Constitution, and the laws of the Confederate *Supreme law.*
States, made in pursuance thereof, and all treaties made, or
which shall be made under the authority of the Confederate
States, shall be the supreme law of the land; and the
judges in every State shall be bound thereby, anything in
the Constitution or laws of any State to the contrary notwithstanding.

4. The Senators and Representatives before mentioned, *Oath to support the constitution required.*
and the members of the several State Legislatures, and all
executive and judicial officers, both of the Confederate
States, and of the several States, shall be bound by oath
or affirmation, to support this constitution; but no religious
test shall ever be required as a qualification to any office
or public trust under the Confederate States.

5. The enumeration, in the Constitution, of certain rights, shall not be construed to deny or disparage others retained by the people of the several States.

Reserved rights of the States

6. The powers not delegated to the Confederate States by the Constitution, nor prohibited by it to the States, are reserved to the States, respectively, or to the people thereof.

ARTICLE VII.

Federal ratification

1. The ratification of the convention of five States shall be sufficient for the establishment of this Constitution between the States so ratifying the same.

Duties of Provisional Congress.

2. When five States shall have ratified this Constitution, in the manner before specified, the Congress under the Provisional Constitution, shall prescribe the time for holding the election of President and Vice-President; and, for the meeting of the Electorial College; and, for counting the votes, and inaugurating the President. They shall, also, prescribe the time for holding the first election for members of Congress under this Constitution, and the time for assembling the same. Until the assembling of such Congress, the Congress under the Provisional Constitution shall continue to exercise the legislative powers granted them; not extending beyond the time limited by the Constitution of the Provisional Government. [*Ratified the 19th day of June,* 1861.]

[No. 12.] RESOLUTIONS CALLING UPON COMPTROLLER FOR STATEMENT OF TAXES FOR THE FIVE YEARS PRECEDING JANUARY, 1860.

Tabular statement required.

Resolved, That the Comptroller be directed to lay before this Convention a tabular statement exhibiting the Public taxes paid into the Treasury of the State from each county, for the five years preceding the 1st day of January, 1860, distinguishing the several subjects from which such taxes were derived, and the amounts received from each subject respectively, in each successive year.

Resolved, That the Comptroller be and he is hereby authorized to employ such additional clerical force as may be necessary to enable him to furnish the foregoing information at an early period. [*Ratified the 20th day of June,* 1861.]

AN ORDINANCE PROVIDING FOR COMPENSA- [No. 13.]
TION TO SHERIFFS FOR HOLDING ELECTIONS
·.FOR. DELEGATES TO THIS CONVENTION.

Be it ordained, &c., That the Sheriffs of the several Compensation to Sheriffs. counties in this State are entitled to, and hereby allowed the same compensation for holding the late elections for delegates to this Convention as they are now allowed by law for holding elections for members of the General Assembly, and the Treasurer be, and he is hereby directed to allow the same to the Sheriffs in the settlement' of their accounts. [*Ratified the 20th day of June,* 1861.]

AN ORDINANCE TO AMEND THE 4TH SECTION [No. 14.]
OF THE 4TH ARTICLE OF THE AMENDMENTS
TO THE CONSTITUTION.

Be it ordained by this Convention of the people, and it Inserts "Confederate" in *is hereby ordained by the authority of the same,* That the lieu of the "United" States fourth section of the fourth article of the amendments to the Constitution, proposed and ratified in the year eighteen hundred and thirty-five, be amended by striking out the word United and inserting in lieu thereof the word Confederate before the word States. [*Ratified the 20th day of June,* 1861.]

[No. 15.] RESOLUTION TOUCHING THE COMPENSATION OF THE PRINTERS TO THIS CONVENTION.

Resolved, That the Secretary of State be and he is hereby directed to make settlement with the Printers to this Convention under the same laws and regulations as govern his settlements with the State Printer. [*Ratified the 20th day of June,* 1861.]

[No. 16.] AN ORDINANCE TO RATIFY THE CONSTITUTION OF THE PROVISIONAL GOVERNMENT OF THE CONFEDERATE STATES OF AMERICA.

We, the people of North Carolina, in Convention assembled, do declare and ordain, and it is hereby declared and ordained, That the State of North Carolina does hereby assent to, and ratify the Constitution for the Provisional Government of the Confederate States of America, adopted at Montgomery, in the State of Alabama, on the 8th day of February, A. D., 1861, by the Convention of Delegates from the States of South Carolina, Georgia, Florida, Alabama, Mississippi and Louisiana, and that North Carolina will enter into the federal association of the States upon the terms therein proposed when admitted by the Congress or any competent authority of the Confederate States.

Done at Raleigh, the twentieth day of May, in the year of our Lord, one thousand eight hundred and sixty-one. [*Ratified the 20th day of June,* 1861.]

[No. 17.] A RESOLUTION TO RAISE AN ADDITIONAL BATTALION OF CAVALRY.

Resolved, That in additional to the Regiment of Cavalry at present authorized to be formed for service during the war, the Governor be authorized to receive such other

companies as have tendered or may hereafter tender their
services for the same period, not exceeding five troops or a
half regiment, and that they be officered in like manner as
the said Regiment of Cavalry herein referred to. [*Ratified the* 21st day of June, 1861.]

RESOLUTION TO FILL A VACANCY IN THE [No. 18.]
CONVENTION.

Resolved, That the President of this Convention issue a
writ to the Sheriff of Bladen county, instructing him to
hold an election in said county on the first Thursday in
August next, for the purpose of electing a delegate to fill
a vacancy in this Convention caused by the resignation of
T. D. McDowell, Esq. [*Ratified the* 21st day of June,
1861.]

RESOLUTION AUTHORIZING THE RAISING OF [No. 19.]
RECRUITS FOR THE 1st REGIMENT OF NORTH
CAROLINA VOLUNTEERS.

Resolved, That the Governor be. and he is hereby
authorized and directed to receive into service, and to arm
and equip, on application of the recruiting officers appointed by the Colonel of the 1st Regiment of North Carolina Volunteers, all such Volunteers as the said recruiting
officers may obtain for their respective companies ; the
said recruits to be received and sworn in for the same
length of time and subject to the same regulations as the
original privates in the respective companies for which
they are recruited are now bound for. [*Ratified the* 22nd
day of June, 1861.]

[No. 20.] AN ORDINANCE IN RELATION TO A STATE FLAG.

Be it ordained by this Convention, and it is hereby ordained by the authority of the same, That the Flag of North Carolina shall consist of a red field with a white star in the centre, and with the inscription, above the star, in a semi-circular form, of "May 20th, 1775," and below the star, in a semi-circular form, "May 20th, 1861." That there shall be two bars of equal width, and the length of the field shall be equal to the bar, the width of the field being equal to both bars: the first bar shall be blue, and the second be white; and the length of the Flag shall be one-third more than its width. [*Ratified the 22nd day of June,* 1861.]

[No. 21.] RESOLUTION IN RELATION TO THE DEPOSIT AND PUBLICATION OF THE ORDINANCES OF THE CONVENTION.

Resolved, That the Secretary of this Convention deposit in the office of the Secretary of State, for safe keeping, all the Ordinances and Resolutions passed by the Convention having the force and effect of laws; and the Secretary of the State shall cause the same to be published in three newspapers published in the City of Raleigh; and he is authorized to contract for said publication at reasonable rates; the expense thereof shall be paid as other public printing; and it shall be sufficient for him to furnish one certified copy only (for which he shall be paid the same fee as for certifying the acts of the General Assembly,) to one of the newspapers, and a printed copy to the others. [*Ratified the 24th day of June,* 1861.]

[No. 22.] AN ORDINANCE IN RELATION TO TAXATION.

SECTION 1. *Be it ordained,* That the third section of the fourth article of the amendments of the Constitution be and the same is hereby annulled.

SEC. 2. *Be it further ordained,* That all free males over the age of twenty-one years and under the age of forty-five years, shall be subject to a capitation tax, not less than the tax laid on land of the value of three hundred dollars, and no other free person nor slave shall be liable to such taxation ; and also land and slaves shall be taxed according to their value, and the tax on slaves shall be as much but not more than that on land according to their respective values; but the tax on slaves may be laid on their general average value in the State, or on their value in classes in respect to age, sex, and other distinctive properties, in the discretion of the General Assembly, and the value be assessed in such modes as may be prescribed by law: *Provided,* That nothing herein contained shall prevent the exemption from taxation of soldiers in the public service, or of free males or slaves, in cases of bodily or mental infirmity, or of such real estate as hath hitherto been exempted by law. [*Ratified the 25th day of June,* 1861.]

Subjects of Capitation tax.

Subjects of Advalorem tax.

AN ORDINANCE TO PROVIDE FOR THE PAYMENT OF THE MILITIA WHILE IN ACTIVE SERVICE.

[No. 23.]

Be it ordained by the Delegates of the people in Convention assembled, and it is hereby ordained by the authority of the same, That the Militia who have been or may be called into the service of the State by the Governor, shall, while in actual service, receive the pay allowed by law to volunteers. [*Ratified the 26th day of June,* 1861.]

Pay the same as that of volunteers.

RESOLUTION IN FAVOR OF THE DOORKEEPERS. [No. 24.]

Resolved, That the Public Treasurer be and he is authorized to pay the Principal and Assistant Doorkeepers of this Convention the sum of fifty dollars each, as extra compensation for the hire of servants. [*Ratified the 26th day of June,* 1861.]

Pays $50 each.

[No. 25.] RESOLUTION AUTHORIZING THE PRESIDENT TO ISSUE WRITS OF ELECTION TO FILL VACANCIES.

Resolved, That the Preisdent of this Convention, or in case of his death, and one of the five delegates authorized in that event to call a session of the Convention, be, and he is hereby authorized and empowered, during the recess thereof, to receive the resignation of delegates, and to issue writs of election to supply vacancies thus created in such manner and at such times as to him shall seem meet; and in like manner to issue writs of elections in case of the death of any member of the Convention, in the recess, the Sheriff of the County certifying the death of the member. [*Ratified the 26th day of June*, 1861.]

[No. 26.] RESOLUTION ASKING INFORMATION FROM THE GOVERNOR.

Resolved, That the Governor be requested to 'communicate' to the Convention, at as early a day as practicable, a list of the appointments to office made by him since the third Monday of November, 1860: whether by and with the advice and consent of the Military Board or otherwise; the dates of such appointments, and under what laws made: the manner, pay and rank of each officer, and also what appointments it will be incumbent on the Executive to make under laws of the General Assembly passed at the last regular and special session.

Resolved, That if necessary, the Governor may employ such additional clerical force as may be necessary to furnish said information. [*Ratified the 26th day of June*, 1861.]

RESOLUTION EXEMPTING VOLUNTEERS FROM [No. 27.] PAYING POLL TAX.

Resolved, That the Volunteers and State troops ten- Exempts all
dered, accepted and employed in the public service, at any prior to 15th August, 1861.
time prior to the 15th August, 1861, shall be exempt from
the payment of free poll taxes for which they are now
responsible. and shall not be compelled to list a taxable
free white poll for this year ; and the Sheriffs shall be
allowed the amount of such exemptions in the settlement
of their respective public accounts, by filing with the Clerk
of the County Court a list, under oath, of the names of
such volunteers and State troops, and it shall be the duty
of the clerks of the several County Courts to certify to
the Comptroller, under their seal of office, the list of polls
so filed with them. [*Ratified the 26th day of June,* 1861.]

RESOLUTION TO RESCIND A RESOLUTION IN [No. 28.] REGARD TO ADJOURNMENT.

Resolved, That the resolution heretofore passed, providing for a recess of this Convention this evening at 7 o'clock,
be, and the same is hereby rescinded, and that this Convention will adjourn on Friday next at 2 o'clock, P. M.,
and will meet again on the 3rd Monday in November next,
unless sooner convened by the President, or by Thomas
Ruffin, of Alamance ; William A. Graham, of Orange ;
Bedford Brown, of Caswell ; James W. Osborne, of Mecklenburg ; and Asa Biggs, of Martin ; members of the Convention, or any three of them, in case of his death.
[*Ratified the 26th day of June,* 1861.]

[No. 29.] AN ORDINANCE TO CEDE TO THE CONFEDE-
RATE STATES, THE PROPERTY IN AND
JURISDICTION OVER THE FORTS, LIGHT
HOUSES, BEACONS, MARINE HOSPITALS AND
MINT IN NORTH CAROLINA.

Cedes jurisdiction over the real estate. SECTION 1. *Be it ordained by the Delegates of the people of North Carolina, in Convention asssembled,* That the property in all tracts or parcels of land, lately held by the United States within the limits of North Carolina, on which were erected any fortification, light houses, beacons, or marine hospitals, and also the lot in the town of Charlotte, in the county of Mecklenburg, on which is situated the buildings of the Mint, be and the same are hereby granted to, and vested in the Confederate States of America, for the like objects, uses, and purposes, for which they were formerly held by the said United States, to have and to hold the same to the said Confederate States so long as they shall severally be devoted and applied to such objects, uses and purposes, and no longer.

Grants other property. SEC. 2. *Be it further ordained by the authority aforesaid,* That all armaments, furniture and machinery at or in any of such fortifications, light houses, beacons, marine hospitals, or mint, are hereby granted to, and vested in the said Confederate States, for the objects, uses, and upon the conditions aforesaid.

Jurisdiction granted. SEC. 3. *Be it further ordained,* That the jurisdiction of the State of North Carolina, over each and all of said tracts or parcels of land, and the buildings situate thereon, is hereby granted to the said Confederate States of America, *Reservation.* excepting and reserving to this State the power to execute within, and upon the same, civil process in all cases, and such criminal process as may issue under her authority against persons charged with offences committed without the limits of said tracts or parcels of land; such jurisdiction to be retained by the said Confederate States, so long as the said tracts or parcels of land shall be used for the purposes hereinbefore expressed, and no longer. [*Ratified the 27th day of June,* 1861.]

AN ORDINANCE TO PROVIDE FOR THE DIS- [No. 30.]
POSITION OF THE STATE TROOPS AND
VOLUNTEERS RAISED UNDER THE ACTS OF
THE GENERAL ASSEMBLY, RESPECTIVELY,
ENTITLED, "AN ACT TO RAISE TEN THOU-
SAND STATE TROOPS," RATIFIED THE 8TH
DAY OF MAY, AND "AN ACT TO PROVIDE
FOR THE PUBLIC DEFENCE," RATIFIED THE
10TH DAY OF MAY, 1861, AND FOR OTHER
PURPOSES. ·

1. *Be it ordained by the Delegates of the people of North Carolina in Convention assembled,* That the State troops levied under the act of the General Assembly, first aforesaid, which have been formed into regiments, with proper complements of officers and men, be, and the same are hereby transferred, by regiments, to the Confederate States of America, upon the same terms and conditions as if they had been raised under the authority of the said Confederate States. *(Transfers State troops to the Confederate States.)*

2. *Be it further ordained by the authority aforesaid,* That all levying and recruiting of troops under said act shall cease and determine from and after the 20th day of August next; and that all troops which shall have been raised under said act prior to that day, shall be organized into regiments and transferred to the Confederate States in the manner and upon the terms and conditions aforesaid. And if there shall be an excess in the number of said troops, sufficient to form a battalion, companies or company, such excess may be organized according to its appropriate numbers, and transferred in like manner. *(Recruiting for State troops to cease August 20th.)*

3. *Be it further ordained,* That all appointments of officers under said act, either in the line or in the staff, over and above the number appropriate to and required by the regiments, battalions and companies thus organized, shall cease and be vacated on the said 20th day of August next; and that His Excellency, the Governor, may, in his discretion, order any Quartermaster, Commissary or Med- *(Commissions of officers not in service to cease August 20th.)*

ical stores, owned by the State, and not required for immediate use, to be turned over to the said Confederate States upon proper receipts for the articles thus delivered, to be taken by the officers accountable for the same.

Officers in service to be retained.

4. *Be it further ordained,* That all commissions to officers in the aforesaid State troops, issued by the Governor and Military Board, under the authority of the act of the General Assembly to create a Military Board, ratified the 10th day of May, 1861, who shall remain in service after the 20th day of August next, as aforesaid, are hereby ratified and confirmed, notwithstanding any provision in the Constitution of the State for a different mode of appointment.

Transfer of Naval forces and vessels.

5. *Be it further ordained,* That the naval forces and vessels of the State be transferred to the Confederate States, upon the same terms and conditions that are provided as to State troops, in the second section of this ordinance, the said vessels to be paid for or accounted for upon terms to be agreed upon by the Governor with the Confederate States ; and that after the 20th day of August next, all naval officers of this State shall be discharged, and all vessels of the navy not accepted by the Confederate States,

Preamble.

shall be sold under the direction of the Governor. And whereas, the President of the Confederate States, through a communication from the Secretary of War, has informed this Convention that he will accept from this State into the service of the Confederate States, two thousand volunteers for twelve months, in addition to the four regiments already in service, and cannot accept any greater number of volunteers for twelve months :

Authorizes the discharge of all volunteers enlisted over or six regiments.

6. *Be it therefore ordained by the authority aforesaid,* That all volunteers who have been called out by the order of the Governor for twelve months, over and above the four regiments aforesaid and two thousand men, to be designated by the Governor, and tendered to the President for service as aforesaid, shall be discharged on the 20th of

Proviso.

August next : *Provided,* That any of said volunteers who shall signify their desire to enlist in the State troops aforesaid or in any corps that may be called for by the President in the mean time, shall be discharged forthwith, to the end that they may enter such new service; and *Provided further*, That the Governor shall again tender such volunteers by regiments to the President of the Confederate States, and if the President shall agree to accept them or any part of them, by, or before the 20th day of August next, it shall be the duty of the Governor to order them, or as many of them as the President shall accept, into the service of the Confederate States, and discharge only the residue: *Provided, further*, That any volunteers discharged as aforesaid, shall, in addition to their pay, be allowed reasonable expenses for traveling to their several homes; and *Provided further*, That the Governor may order out the Militia as volunteers or otherwise, in case of invasion or imminent danger thereof.

7. *Be it further ordained*, That all provisions of the aforesaid acts of the Assembly, authorizing the raising of a greater number of men, or of a different species of force than is hereinbefore comprehended, or as are otherwise inconsistent with this ordinance, are hereby repealed and declared of no effect. *Repeals act of General Assembly.*

8. *Be it further ordained*, That the act of the General Assembly entitled "An act to create a Military Board," be, and the same is hereby repealed from and after the 20th day of August next: *Provided*, That the office of Military Secretary shall be continued until the 20th day of September next, for the purpose of settling the military accounts. *Act creating Military Board repealed.*

9. *Be it further ordained*, That no oath shall be required to be taken by the officers or soldiers of any of the forces aforesaid, except the oath of allegiance to the State of North Carolina, prior to their being mustered into the service of the Confederate States; but each man shall be held and deemed to be in the military service and subject to the rules and articles of war of the Confederate States from the time of his signing the articles of enlistment. *No oath to be required of soldiers except oath of allegiance to N. C.*

10. *Be it further ordained*, That it shall be the duty of the Governor to take immediate measures, and issue the

necessary orders to carry into effect the foregoing provisions of this ordinance.

General Assem
bly may amend
modify or repeal

11. *Be it further ordained,* That this ordinance may be
amended, modified or repealed by the General Assembly,
so far as regards the discharge of the twelve months volunteers which may not have been accepted by the government of the Confederate States. [*Ratified the 27th day of
June,* 1861.]

[No. 31.] AN ORDINANCE TO SECURE TO CERTAIN OFFICERS AND SOLDIERS THE RIGHT TO VOTE.

Authorizes sol
diers to vote

SECTION 1. *Be it ordained by this Convention and it is
hereby ordained by authority of the same,* That all officers
and soldiers in the service of the State, or of the Confederate States, who are of the age of twenty-one years, and
who are citizens of this State, or who, if within the State,
shall be absent from their respective counties at elections
hereafter to be held, if the exigencies of the times shall
permit, shall be entitled to vote for Sheriffs, Clerks of the
County and Superior Courts, and members of the General
Assembly for their respective counties; and shall also be
entitled to vote for Governor, Electors for President and
Vice-President of the Confederate States, and for members of the Confederate Congress for their respective districts.

Three freehold
ers to open the
polls

SEC. 2. *Be it further ordained,* That three free-holders
of the respective companies, under the direction of the
commanding officers of the regiments to which they belong,
shall open polls on Thursday before the day appointed for
holding elections in this State, and said elections shall be
conducted in all respects according to the laws of this
State. The three free-holders aforesaid shall prepare a
fair copy of the votes polled, and shall transmit the same
with the list of voters to the Sheriffs of their respective
counties; and where officers and soldiers in the same com-

panies shall vote in different counties or different Congres-
sional districts, the said free-holders shall specify accordingly, and make returns to the Sheriffs of the different
counties above referred to.

SEC. 3. *Be it further ordained,* That the Sheriffs of the respective counties of this State shall count the votes of the said officers and soldiers, if received within seven days after the elections; and they shall not declare the result of the said election until the seven days above mentioned shall have expired.

SEC. 4. *Be it further ordained,* That this ordinance shall be in force from and after the day of its ratification : *Provided,* This ordinance shall be in force during the existence of the present war with the United States and no longer.   [*Ratified the 25th day of June,* 1861.]

RESOLUTION ORDERING THE ORDINANCES TO BE PRINTED IN PAMPHLET FORM. [No. 32.]

Ordered, That the Secretary cause five hundred copies of all the Ordinances and Resolutions having the force of laws adopted at this session, to be printed in pamphlet form ; the said ordinances and resolutions to be inserted in the order of their dates, and in the form in which they stand enrolled : Two copies of the same to be distributed to each member of the Convention, one to each of the officers ; twenty-five to be deposited in the office of the Secretary of State ; ten to be delivered to the Clerk of the Supreme Court for the use of the Court ; one to each of the Superior Court Judges and solicitors ; the residue to be retained, subject to further order.   *Ratified the 27th day of June,* 1861.]

6

[No. 33.] RESOLUTION IN FAVOR OF THE W., C. & R. RAILROAD COMPANY.

Requires Governor to execute and deliver bonds heretofore authorized

Resolved, That His Excellency, the Governor, be requested, and the Treasurer be directed, to execute and deliver to the Wilmington, Charlotte and Rutherford Railroad Company, the amount of coupon State bonds to which the said corporation was entitled on the 1st day of April last, for work before that time accomplished: *Provided,* The same shall be accepted by the said corporation at their par value: *Provided.* This resolution shall not be construed to authorize or direct the Governor and Treasurer to issue any other State bonds to any other corporation in in this State, unless, in his judgment, he may consider it his duty to do so under the requirements of law. [*Ratified the 28th day of June,* 1861.]

[No. 34.] AN ORDINANCE TO PROVIDE THE WAYS AND MEANS FOR THE DEFENCE OF THE STATE.

Appropriates $3,200,000

SECTION 1. *Be it ordained, &c.,* That the sum of three millions two hundred thousand dollars, or so much thereof as may be necessary, be, and the same is hereby appropriated to meet the demands on the Public Treasury for the next ensuing two years, which sum shall be raised and provided for in the way and manner following:

$200,000 to be issued in notes of 10, 25 and 50 cents

SEC. 2. *Be it further ordained,* That the Public Treasurer is hereby authorized and required to have suitably prepared, and to issue Treasury notes, payable to bearer, upon the faith and credit of the State, to the amount of two hundred thousand dollars, of the various denominations of ten, twenty-five and fifty cents, in the following proportions, to-wit: forty thousand dollars in notes or bills of ten cents, sixty thousand dollars in bills or notes of twenty-five cents, and one hundred thousand dollars in notes or bills of fifty cents, which said notes shall be receivable in payment of public dues: shall bear no interest:

shall be made payable to bearer, and be signed by the public Treasurer, or by some person to be by him duly authorized and appointed to sign the same, and who shall receive a reasonable compensation for such service, to be paid out of the Public Treasury, and shall be redeemable on or before the first day of January, 1866 : *Provided, however,* That no such notes shall be issued before the first day of March next, and that the General Assembly may make provision for the redemption of said notes before the time specified, or may extend the time of redemption, as in their judgment the public may require. The Public Treasurer and Comptroller shall each provide a book in which shall be kept an accurate account of all the notes of the various denominations paid out under the provisions of this ordinance, and also an accurate account of all sums returned to the Treasury ; which books shall at all times be open to the inspection of the General Assembly, and for the keeping of such books, they may, if absolutely necessary, be allowed to employ some suitable person to act as clerk.

SEC. 3. *Be it further ordained,* That the Public Treasurer of the State be, and he is hereby authorized and directed to negotiate a loan or loans, with the several banks of this State, or with private individuals, in such sums and at such times as he may deem necessary and proper, to an amount not exceeding, in the aggregate, the sum of three millions of dollars, including the amount already borrowed of the banks of this State, under the provisions of an act passed at the last session of the General Assembly, entitled "An Act to provide ways and means for the public defence"—for which the said Public Treasurer shall issue the bonds of the State bearing six per cent. interest, and payable twelve months after the date thereof: and should the Public Treasurer not be prepared to pay the same at maturity, he is hereby authorized to renew the same on such terms and for such times as he may think proper, or to negotiate new loans in lieu thereof, and he, the Public Treasurer, shall keep a true and accurate account of all such loans, and make report thereof to the General Assembly from time to time.

(margin note:) Public Treasurer to borrow from the Banks $3,000,000, and to issue State Bonds for the same.

Authorises the Banks to issue bills of the denomination of $1, $2 and $2½, upon certain conditions.

SEC. 4. *Be it further ordained*, That those banks in this State who shall loan to the State their *pro rata* amount of the sum hereby authorized to be borrowed of them, whose charters forbid their issuing bills of a less denomination than five dollars, be, and they are hereby authorized to issue bills of the denominations of one dollar, two dollars, and two dollars and a half, to the extent of five per cent. of their capital stock actually paid in: *Provided*, That the same shall not be construed to authorize the said banks to issue an aggregate amount of circulation greater than that now authorized by their charter. This authority hereby granted to issue bills of the denominations of one dollar, two dollars, and two dollars and a half shall cease whenever the General Assembly shall provide and direct, upon the payment to the banks, the principal and interest of the sums borrowed of them under the provisions of this ordinance.

Resumption of specie payments not required of banks lending money to the State.

SEC. 5. *Be it further ordained*, That no bank of this State shall be required to resume specie payments, whilst any portion of the amounts herein authorized to be borrowed from such banks shall remain unpaid.

Punishment of counterfeiters.

SEC. 6. *Be it further ordained*, That if any person falsely make, forge or counterfeit, or cause the same to be done, or willingly aid or assist therein, any Treasury note in imitation of, or purporting to be a Treasury note or bond issued by authority of this act, with the intent to defraud the State, or corporations or other persons; the person so offending shall be deemed guilty of felony, and on conviction thereof in the Superior Court, he shall be adjudged to stand in the pillory one hour and receive thirty-nine lashes on his bare back, and be imprisoned not less than six months, nor more than three years, and fined at the discretion of the court, and all or any of such punishments may, at the discretion of the court, be inflicted.

SEC. 7. *Be it further ordained*, That if any person, either directly or indirectly, whether for the sake of gain, or with intent to defraud or injure any other person, shall utter or publish any false, forged, or counterfeit notes as mentioned in the preceding section, or shall pass or deliver, or attempt to pass or deliver, the same to another person, knowing the same to be falsely forged or counterfeited, the person so offending shall, on conviction thereof in the Superior Court, be punished in like manner as is provided in the preceding section of this ordinance.

SEC. 8. *Be it further ordained,* That this ordinance, or any portion of it, may hereafter be altered, modified or repealed by the General Assembly, provided nothing contained in this section shall be construed to divest any rights accruing to the banks or other parties without their consent. *(margin: Authority granted the General Assembly.)*

SEC. 9. *Be it further ordained,* That the act passed at the late session of the General Assembly, entitled, "An Act to provide ways and means for the public defence," ratified the 11th day of May, 1861, be, and the same is hereby abrogated and annulled. [*Ratified the 28th day of June,* 1861.] *(margin: Annuls act of General Assembly.)*

AN ORDINANCE TO AMEND AN ORDINANCE [No. 35.] PASSED AT THE PRESENT SESSION OF THIS CONVENTION, ENTITLED "AN ORDINANCE TO PROVIDE FOR A BOARD OF CLAIMS."

Be it ordained, That the ordinance passed at the present session, entitled "An ordinance to provide for a Board of Claims," ratified on the 8th day of June, 1861, be, and the same is hereby so amended and modified as to provide that the said Board of Claims, shall report the result of their action on such claims as they may allow, to the General Assembly, at its next session, and that the General Assembly is hereby authorized to pass finally on such allowed claims, and make provision for their immediate payment, and that all such claims as may not be reported to and passed upon by the General Assembly, shall be reported to the Convention at its adjourned session in November, for the final action of said Convention. [*Ratified the 28th day of June,* 1861.] *(margin: Board of Claims to report to the General Assembly.)*

ORDINANCES AND RESOLUTIONS

PASSED BY

THE STATE CONVENTION

OF

NORTH CAROLINA.

𝔖𝔢𝔠𝔬𝔫𝔡 𝔖𝔢𝔰𝔰𝔦𝔬𝔫 𝔦𝔫 𝔑𝔬𝔳𝔢𝔪𝔟𝔢𝔯 𝔞𝔫𝔡 𝔇𝔢𝔠𝔢𝔪𝔟𝔢𝔯, 1861.

RALEIGH:
JOHN W. SYME, PRINTER TO THE CONVENTION.
1862.

ORDINANCES AND RESOLUTIONS

OF THE

STATE CONVENTION

OF

NORTH CAROLINA.

SECOND SESSION IN NOVEMBER AND DECEMBER, 1861.

--

RESOLUTION TO TRANSMIT A COPY OF THE [No. 1.]
SUPREME COURT REPORTS TO THE DEPART-
MENT OF JUSTICE OF THE CONFEDERATE
STATES.

Resolved, That the State Librarian transmit to the **Supreme Court Reports.**
department of justice of the Confederate States of America
one set of the Reports of the Supreme Court of this State,
if the same be in the Public Library, or that he purchase
such as may be deficient, for that purpose.

RESOLUTION RELATIVE TO THE DAILY SIT- [No. 2.]
TINGS OF THIS CONVENTION.

Resolved, That from and after to-day this Convention **Alters hours of sitting.**
will meet daily at ten o'clock and adjourn at two o'clock,
re-assemble again at four o'clock and adjourn at its discretion. [*Ratified the 8th day of December,* 1861.]

7

[No. 3.] AN ORDINANCE TO AUTHORIZE THE PUBLIC
TREASURER TO EMPLOY AN ADDITIONAL
CLERK IN THE TREASURY DEPARTMENT,
AND OTHER PURPOSES.

Be it ordained, That until it shall be otherwise enacted
by the General Assembly, the salary of the Clerk of the
Treasury Department be increased to twelve hundred dollars annually, and that the Public Treasurer be authorized
to employ a second clerk in that department, and that his
salary shall be seven hundred and fifty dollars annually,
and that the Comptroller be authorized to employ a clerk
in his office, and that his salary be the sum of seven hundred and fifty dollars annually, and this increase of the
said salaries shall commence from and after the 1st day of
January, 1862. [*Ratified the 9th day of November,* 1861.]

[No. 4.] RESOLUTION IN FAVOR OF DR. WM. E. POOL.

Resolved, That the Governor be, and he is hereby authorized and required to instruct the Paymaster to pay to Dr.
William E. Pool, of Murfreesboro', taken prisoner at Hatteras, and now at Fort Wayne, or to his authorized agent,
the compensation of an assistant surgeon, from the first of
July, 1861, until such time as he shall be released or
exchanged. [*Ratified the 6th day of December,* 1861.]

[No. 5.] AN ORDINANCE TO TRANSFER CERTAIN COM-
PANIES TO COL. GREEN'S REGIMENT.

Be it ordained, That the Governor of this State be, and
he is hereby authorized, if he shall deem it expedient, to
transfer to Col. Green's Regiment of Volunteers, the two
companies now at High Point, under the command of Captains Cook and Sharp: *Provided,* That Capt. Cook shall

first return to the Governor or the Adjutant General of
this State, all such public monies and orders for public
money, as he has heretofore received for the purchase of
guns: *And, provided further*, That the said companies
shall not be so transferred unless all the officers, non-commissioned officers and privates of said companies shall first
signify their assent thereto in writing. [*Ratified the 6th
day of December*, 1861.]

RESOLUTIONS OF CONFIDENCE IN OUR CAUSE [No. 6.]
OF WAR, AND IN THE PRESIDENT AND
ARMY.

Resolved, That we, the delegates of the people of North   Express undiminished confi-
Carolina, in Convention assembled, entertain an undimin- dence.
ished confidence in the justice of the cause for which we
have taken up arms, and we hold it to be the duty of the
people of these Southern States to maintain and uphold
that cause with all the means they can command.

Resolved, That in behalf of the people of North Caro- No sacrifice can
cause us to
lina, we declare to our sister States of this Confederacy, desist.
and to the world, that no measure of loss, no sacrifice of
life or property, no privation or want, or suffering, shall
cause us to shrink from the performance of our whole duty
in the achievement of our independence.

Resolved, That from the cruel and barbarous manner in Barbarity of
the enemy.
which our enemies have carried on this war—a war in which
aged and dignified men and helpless women have been
seized, and without accusation or warrant of authority, cast
into prison—in which private property has been wantonly
destroyed—in which robbery and arson are principal means
of aggression, and in which servile insurrection has been
proclaimed: we are convinced that there is a radical
incompatibility between such a people and our ourselves:
that from them our separation is final, and for the indepen
dence we have asserted, we will accept no alternative.

Resolved. That we have full confidence in the wisdom, integrity and patriotism of the President of the Confederate States, and we congratulate him and our whole country upon the success with which he has administered the Government.

Resolved. That to the officers and soldiers who have gone forth to meet the dangers of this war, we are under a deep debt of gratitude for the valor and fortitude with which they have defended us from the assaults of our enemies and illustrated the glory of our arms.

Resolved. That a copy of these resolutions be sent to our Representatives in Congress, with a request that they be communicated to his Excellency, the President of the Confederate States, and to Congress. [*Ratified the 6th day of December, 1861.*]

[No. 7.] RESOLUTION REQUESTING OUR SENATORS AND REPRESENTATIVES IN CONGRESS TO VOTE FOR AN INCREASE OF THE PAY OF SOLDIERS.

Resolved, That our Senators and Representatives in the Confederate Congress, be requested to vote for an increase of the pay of the common soldiers of the Confederate army: *Provided,* The resources of the Confederate Treasury will justify it.

[No. 8.] AN ORDINANCE IN REGARD TO THE SUPPLY OF SALT.

1. *Be it ordained by the Delegates of the people of North Carolina, in Convention assembled, and it is hereby ordained by the authority of the same,* That a Commissioner be appointed by this Convention to manufacture salt for the use of the people of this State, at such place or places as he shall judge best: and that he furnish it to the people of

each county at the most convenient depot on the railroad to such county, or some navigable waters, on the payment of the cost of manufacturing and transportation; which price shall be paid on the delivery of the salt.

2. *Be it further ordained,* That the said Commissioner shall have full power to employ the necessary agents and laborers, and to contract for materials, in the name of the State, necessary in carrying out the provisions of this ordinance, and to draw upon the Public Treasurer, from time to time, therefor, not exceeding the sum of one hundred thousand dollars.

Appropriates $100,000.

3. *Be it further ordained,* That it shall be the duty of said Commissioner to proceed as soon as practicable to the discharge of this duty, and as salt can be made, it be sent forward to the various depots on the several railroads of the State. or on some navigable waters, for the accommodation of every section of the State, equally, and in such order as he may find best to meet the wants of the country.

To enter upon duties as soon as practicable.

4. *Be it further ordained,* That Justices of the Peace of the several counties in this State, a majority being present, may meet at the Court House, in term time, or in vacation of the courts, and make such order as they may prefer, touching the delivering, distribution and payment for the salt manufactured for the use of the people of such county, and to that end may advance the money out of the Treasury of the county, or otherwise: *Provided,* That they shall not allow the salt to be sold in speculation, or for more than the actual cost.

Duties of Justices of the Peace

5. *Be it further ordained,* That it shall not be lawful for any one to purchase more of the salt so made, than he requires for his own use, or for distribution. at the cost and expense of transportation, and if any one shall purchase any salt so made and re-sell it for a profit, he shall be guilty of a misdemeanor, and on conviction thereof in any of the County or Superior Courts, shall be fined or imprisoned at the discretion of the court.

Speculation forbidden.

6. *Be a further ordained.* That this ordinance shall continue in force and operation during the continuance of the present war, unless the Legislature shall otherwise order.

7. *Be it further ordained.* That if the Commissioner should die or remove from the State, resign or refuse to act, or should prove faithless to the trust reposed in him, the Convention then not being in session, the Governor shall supply the vacancy created in any of the forementioned means.

8. *Be it further ordained.* That it shall be the duty of the Commissioner to make a report to the Governor every month, showing the progress of the work, its cost, &c. It shall be the duty of said Commissioner on the first Monday of each month, to report to the Governor the quantity of salt manufactured during the month preceding, and the disposition made of all the salt made, the cost of production and transportion, and the income to the State on the salt made and sold, and that the Governor shall lay such reports before the General Assembly at the first session, and they may make such order for change in the management of the business and settlement with the Commissioner as in their wisdom may seem right.

9. *Be it further ordained,* That the Commissioner shall, before entering on the duties of his office, take an oath of office, and give bond payable to the State in the sum of one hundred thousand dollars, with security to be approved by the Governor, and shall take bond and ample security from every agent by him appointed, whose duties shall require him to receive or pay out money, and that all such bonds shall be payable to the State of North Carolina.

10. *Be it further ordained.* That the Commissioner shall receive an annual salary of fifteen hundred dollars, and his traveling expenses. [*Ratified the 6th day of December.* 1861.]

RESOLUTION ON TAKING A RECESS.   [No. 9.]

Resolved, That this Convention will take a recess from and after Friday the 13th instant, until Monday the 20th of January next. [*Ratified the 6th day of December,* 1861.]

AN ORDINANCE CONCERNING THE REPEAL OF [No. 10.] THE FOURTEENTH CHAPTER OF THE ACTS OF THE SECOND EXTRA SESSION OF 1861.

Be it ordained by the Delegates of the people of North Carolina, in Convention assembled, and it is hereby ordained Annuls 14th chapter of the Acts of General Assembly. *by the authority of the same,* That the fourteenth chapter of the acts of the General Assembly, passed at the second extra session, entitled "An act to alter the rules of evidence as applicable to Indians," be and the same is hereby repealed and annulled. [*Ratified the 6th day of December,* 1861.]

A RESOLUTION TO TRANSFER CERTAIN MILI- [No. 11.] TARY COMPANIES TO COL. W. J. GREEN.

Resolved, That the Governor, if he shall deem it proper, be and he is hereby authorized to transfer to Colonel W. J. Green's Independent North Carolina Regiment, such companies as have been accepted and not yet assigned to other regiments, upon their application for such transfer : *Provided,* That no member of a company shall be required to join said service without his consent in writing. [*Ratified the 6th day of December,* 1861.]

[No. 12.] AN ORDINANCE TO PROVIDE FOR AMENDING THE FORTY-SIXTH SECTION OF THE CONSTITUTION OF THIS STATE IN REGARD TO TAKING THE YEAS AND NAYS IN EITHER HOUSE OF THE GENERAL ASSEMBLY.

Be it ordained by the Delegates of the people of North Carolina, in Convention assembled, and it is hereby ordained by the authority of the same, That the forty-sixth section of the Constitution of this State be so amended as to insert, after the word "seconded," in the fourth line of said section, the words "by one-fifth of the members present.' [*Ratified the 6th day of December,* 1861.]

[No. 13.] AN ORDINANCE TO AMEND THE SECOND SECTION OF THE FOURTH ARTICLE OF THE AMENDMENTS TO THE CONSTITUTION.

Be it ordained by the Delegates of the people of North Carolina, in assembled, and it is hereby ordained by the authority of the same, That the second section of the fourth article of the amendments to the Constitution, shall be amended to read as follows: "No person who shall deny the being of God or the divine authority of both the Old and New Testaments, or who shall hold religious opinions incompatible with the freedom or safety of the State, shall be capable of hoding any office or place of trust or profit in the civil department of this State." [*Ratified the 6th day of December,* 1861.]

[No. 14.] RESOLUTION APPOINTING DENNIS D. FEREBEE, Esq.. COMMISSIONER TO RICHMOND.

Resolved, That Dennis D. Ferebee, Esq., be, and he is hereby appointed a Commissioner whose duty it shall be to visit Richmond, and confer with the Secretary of the Confederate Treasury, and with the Congress of the Confederate States, now in session, and ascertain what kind of payment will be accepted, and that on his return, he report the result of said conference to this Convention, for their consideration and action.   [*Ratified the 6th day of December*, 1861.]

RESOLUTION OF THANKS TO THE OFFICERS AND SOLDIERS FOR GALLANT CONDUCT IN DEFENDING HATTERAS.   [No. 15.]

Resolved, That we have undiminished confidence in the courage and loyalty of the officers and soldiers who, after a long and severe bombardment, were compelled to surrender, to an overwhelming force, the inadequate defences at Hatteras, on the twenty-ninth of August last, and that they deserve our thanks for their gallant conduct.   [*Ratified the 3rd day of December*, 1861.]

AN ORDINANCE TO PROVIDE FOR THE RAISING OF MONEY FOR THE SUPPORT OF GOVERNMENT, AND FOR THE ISSUE OF TREASURY NOTES FOR THE PURPOSE OF PAYING THE PUBLIC DEBT, AND PURCHASING SUPPLIES FOR THE MILITARY FORCES EMPLOYED FOR DEFENCE IN THE PRESENT WAR, AND FOR OTHER PURPOSES.   [No. 16.]

1. *Be it ordained by the Delegates of the people of North Carolina, in Convention assembled, and it is hereby ordained by the authority of the same*, That the Public Treasurer is authorized to issue Treasury notes for such sums, not exceeding, at any one time, three millions of dollars, as the exigencies of the public service may require, before or on the first day of January, 1863, and the said notes shall be prepared and signed, and issued as hereinafter provided.

Authorizes the issue of $3,000,000 in Treasury notes.

2 *B. it further ordained*, That the Public Treasurer cause the said notes to be prepared, and that they shall be signed by the Public Treasurer, on behalf of the State, and countersigned by the Comptroller; and each of those officers shall keep, in proper books, separate and accurate accounts, showing the number, date, and amount of each of the said notes signed and countersigned by them respectively, and, also, accounts showing all such of said notes as may be paid or redeemed and cancelled, from time to time, and the said Treasurer shall account, monthly, for all such of said notes as shall have been countersigned by the Comptroller, and delivered to the Treasurer for issue.

3. *Be it further ordained*, That the said Treasury notes shall be payable at the Public Treasury, to the bearer, on the first day of January, 1865, and bear interest from date at the rate of six per cent. per annum, for every hundred dollars, and in that proportion for sums greater or less than one hundred dollars; and the said notes shall be of the several denominations of five dollars, ten dollars, twenty dollars, fifty dollars, one hundred dollars, and two hundred dollars; and in the following proportions, that is to say: notes for five dollars, ten dollars, and twenty dollars, the amount of four hundred thousand dollars of each denomination shall be issued: and notes for fifty dollars, to the amount of eight hundred thousand dollars; and those for one hundred dollars and for two hundred dollars, to the amount of five hundred thousand dollars of each denomination: and in the course of the issuing of said notes, from time to time, the said relative proportions shall be observed as near as may be

4. *Be it further ordained*, That the principal money, and the interest due on the said notes, shall be paid at the maturity thereof to the several lawful holders thereof, upon presentment at the Treasury, out of any money in the Treasury not otherwise appropriated: and, further, that at any time or times before the maturity of said notes, the Treasurer may give notice, in the newspapers printed in Raleigh of his readiness to pay the same on any class or

denomination of said notes, or any certain part thereof, and the interest shall close on the notes designated in such notice at the expiration of forty days after such notice given.

5. *Be it further ordained,* That the said notes may be issued by the Treasurer, in payment of any warrant in favor, of public creditors, or for the purpose of paying military officers and troops in service, or for the purchase of supplies for such troops, and for the payment of coupons upon any bond or bonds hitherto given, or hereafter to be given, or for any other demand upon the Treasury by persons who may be willing to receive the same in payment at par; and the Public Treasurer may borrow money, from time to time, upon the credit of said notes, as the public service may require, not exceeding the said sum of three millions of dollars: *Provided,* That upon such loans interest shall not be charged or paid at a greater rate than six per cent. per annum, and further, that no Treasury notes shall be pledged, nor shall they be sold, or issued for any purpose, for less than the amount due on the same, including interest accrued thereon, if any.

The notes to be paid out by the Public Treasurer.

6. *Be it further ordained,* That the said Treasury notes shall, at any time or times hereafter, be receivable at the Treasury in payment for land entered, and for taxes, and any debt to the State at the Treasury, and in making such payment, the holder shall have credit for the principal money mentioned in said note, and the interest accrued thereon up to the day of payment; and accounts shall be kept, as aforesaid, of the notes thus paid or redeemed, distinguishing the sum allowed for interest from the principal.

The notes good for any debt to the State.

7. *Be it further ordained,* That the said Treasury notes shall be received by Sheriffs, and other collecting officers, in payment of the public taxes in their respective counties, and the said officers so receiving any of the said notes shall, at the time of payment, take from the person paying them a receipt on the back of each note for the amount allowed therefor and the date thereof, and such officer shall keep a distinct and specific account of said notes so received

Sheriffs and collectors to receive them and to all winterest in payment, showing the person from whom received, the number and date, the day on which he received them, and the amount of the principal, and also the interest allowed by him, and deliver the said notes and accounts to the Public Treasurer; and he shall, thereupon, and on his oath to the truth of said account, receive credit for the amount thereof.

8. *Be it further ordained*, That the holders of the Treasury notes issued under the authority of this ordinance, may have the same funded, by request, to the Treasurer, to give in exchange for them bonds of the State, payable in thirty years, at the Public Treasury, and bearing interest at the rate of six per cent. per annum, payable half yearly, with coupons attached, for the interest, payable, also, at the Treasury: *Provided, however*, That such bonds shall be issued for the amount of five hundred dollars, and one thousand dollars only: *And, provided, further*, That upon application for such exchange, the interest upon the Treasury notes shall be allowed up to the first day of January, or April, or July, or October next, preceding the request for such exchange, as the case may be, and the interest on the bonds given in exchange, shall run from the day to which the interest on the notes was allowed; and of the notes received by the Treasurer, and of the bonds given in exchange therefor, full and accurate accounts shall also be kept as aforesaid; and the Public Treasurer is authorized and required to issue such coupon bonds, agreeably to the provisions of the ninetieth chapter of the Revised Code, subject to the restrictions and modifications herein provided.

9. *Be it further ordained*, That the Treasury notes so received at the Treasury, from Sheriffs, and others, as aforesaid, shall not be re-issued, but shall be deemed to be paid, and be cancelled; and other Treasury notes to the same amount and of the same denomination, and payable at the same time and place, with the same rate of interest may, in like manner, be issued in the place of those so redeemed: *Provided, nevertheless*, That the aggregate

amount of said notes outstanding at any one time, and of the bonds given in exchange for notes as aforesaid, shall not exceed the said sum of three millions of dollars of principal money.

10. *Be it further ordained,* That the act of the General Assembly, entitled an act to authorize the Public Treasurer to issue Treasury notes, ratified the twentieth day of September, 1861, be, and the same is hereby amended.

11. *Be it further ordained,* That if any person shall falsely make, forge, or counterfeit, or cause to be made, forged, or counterfeited, any notes, bond, or coupon, in imitation of or purporting to be a Treasury note, or bond, or coupon, made or issued by authority of this ordinance, or shall aid or assist therein, with intent to defraud the State, or any corporation, or person or persons, he or she so offending shall be deemed guilty of felony, and on due conviction thereof, shall be adjudged to stand in the pillory one hour and receive thirty-nine lashes on the bare back, and be imprisoned not less than six months or more than three years, and be fined: and in the discretion of the court, all or any of the said punishments may be inflicted.

12. *Be it further ordained,* That if any person, for the sake of gain, or with the intent to injure or defraud the State, or any corporation or any other person or persons, shall either directly or indirectly utter or publish any false, forged, or counterfeited note, bond, or coupon, as mentioned in the preceding section, or shall pass or deliver, or attempt to pass or deliver the same to any other person, knowing the same to be falsely, forged or counterfeited, he or she so offending shall, on due conviction thereof, be punished in like manner as is provided in the preceding section of this ordinance.

13. *Be it further ordained,* That the Treasurer shall keep and furnish to the Comptroller, an accurate account of the Treasury notes issued, or to be issued by him under act of the General Assembly, and the ordinance heretofore passed and not annulled; and the Comptroller shall also keep an accurate account of all such notes in the same

[marginal notes:]
Amends Act of General Assembly.

Punishment for counterfeiting.

Punishment for circulating counterfeit notes.

Account to be kept.

manner as required herein in relation to the Treasury
notes authorized to be issued by this ordinance.

General Assembly may alter or modify.

14. *Be it further ordained*, That this ordinance may be
altered or modified by the General Assembly, but not so
as to impair the obligation of the said notes, bonds, or
coupons actually issued under the authority of this ordinance, and then held by any person or persons. [*Ratified
the 1st day of December*, 1861.]

[No. 17.] ORDINANCE DIRECTING THE PAYMENT OF CLAIMS, AWARDED BY THE COURT OF CLAIMS.

Board of Claims—Disbursement

*Be it ordained by the Delegates of the people of North
Carolina, in Convention assembled, and it is hereby ordained
by the authority of the same*, That the Treasurer of the
State pay out of any monies in the Public Treasury, not
otherwise appropriated, as follows:

To Paul C. Cameron, two thousand five hundred and
eighty-three dollars;

To Pride Jones, one hundred and ninety-seven dollars
and seventy-three cents;

To Watts, White & Co., forty-six dollars and seventy-
three cents;

To Angelo Garybaldo, one hundred and seventy-seven
dollars and fifty-four cents;

To E. C. Belvin, forty-two dollars and forty-five cents;

To W. H. Bobbitt, three hundred and thirty-six dollars
and forty cents;

To James H. Hambaugh, one hundred and two dollars:

To T. S. Vail, thirty dollars and ten cents;

To T. H. McRorie, one hundred and sixty-four dollars
and ten cents;

To Will. H. Parsley, one thousand one hundred and
twenty-two dollars and fifty-one cents;

To W. H. Mitchell, twenty-five dollars and eighty-three
cents;

To J. R. Shufford, six dollars and twenty-five cents ;   Board of Claims—

To Smith, Stone & Banks, one hundred and forty-nine dollars and seventy-eight cents :   Disbursements

To W. B. Hughes & Bros., two hundred and sixty-four dollars and sixteen cents :

To Willie Simms, thirty dollars and thirty cents :

To J. H. Applewhite, thirty-nine dollars and thirty cents :

To Wyman, Davey & Co., six hundred and forty-eight dollars ;

To W. S. Cason, eighty-three dollars and seven cents :

To Willie Askew, twenty-two dollars and fifty cents ;

To Williams & Haywood, thirty dollars and ninety-two cents ;

To Thos. Harwick, thirty-three dollars and fifty cents ;

To Wilson G. Lamb, one hundred and seventy-one dollars ;

To Jamison, Simonton & Co., five hundred and thirty-two dollars and fifty-six cents :

To McNair, Bro. & Co., ninety-two dollars and thirty-four cents :

To J. L. Baker, two hundred and eighty-five dollars and twenty-five cents :

To R. W. Hamlin, twenty-one dollars and twenty-one cents ;

To D. C. Parks, ass., three hundred and two dollars and ninety-seven cents ;

To J. A. Bryan, twenty-five dollars ;

To Edward Wood, one hundred dollars ;

To C. Perkins & Son, twenty-one dollars ;

To W. C. Brown and Z. B. Vance, one hundred and sixty-four dollars and twenty-eight cents ;

To John Yancey & Son, nine hundred and sixty dollars and fifty-one cents ;

To Joseph Ramsey, ass., twenty-nine dollars and thirty-two cents ;

To F. and H. Fries, one thousand two hundred and sixty-two dollars and fifty-five cents ;

To Capt. John Randolph, three hundred and seventy-four dollars and twenty-five cents ;

To N. C. R. R. Co., five hundred and twelve dollars and twenty-eight cents;

To James S. Snow, fifty-three dollars and ninety-two cents:

To H. J. Evans, sixty-two dollars and seventy-four cents:

To E. L. Lindsey, one thousand six hundred and twenty dollars:

To M. A. Woody, eighty dollars:

To Davidson & Miller, one hundred and ninety dollars and seventy cents;

To T. P. Siler, five hundred and ninety-one dollars and ninety-eight cents:

To L. M. Cook, twenty-five dollars:

To W. W. Happer, sixty-two dollars and twelve cents:

To Joseph W. Stockton, two hundred and ninety-eight dollars and two cents:

To B. L. Perry, sixty-nine dollars and fifty cents:

To W. C. Roberts, ninety dollars:

To C. H. Barnam, eighty-one dollars;

To Gains, Dearer & Co., one thousand nine hundred and forty-four dollars and eighty-seven cents:

To C. N. Meaclos, thirty-five dollars:

To Robt D. Hart, forty-two dollars:

To John T. Barns, one hundred and eighty-one dollars and eighty cents;

To Alfred Everett, seventy-four dollars and seventy-five cents;

To Peter G. Foster, forty dollars:

To John Watts, sixty-one dollars and eighty-three cents:

To Cape Fear Steamboat Co., eight hundred and seven dollars and twenty cents;

To P. F. Pescud, sixty-four dollars and eighty-five cents:

To Lewis B. Erambert, one hundred and ninety-three dollars and thirty-two cents:

To W. A. Graves, eight hundred dollars;

To W. W. Fife, twenty-one dollars and fifty cents;

To Joseph Lawrence, two hundred and thirty-two dollars and thirty cents:

To John P. Nowell, one hundred and eighty dollars and fifty cents ;

To Jacob Backman, one hundred and forty-one dollars and fifty cents ;

To Wm. Smith, thirty dollars ;

To E. Simmons, ten dollars ;

To William Page, forty-six dollars and forty-five cents ;

To James Ward, twenty-two dollars and fifty cents ;

To W. G. Hill, five dollars ;

To Stevenson & Weddell, two hundred and sixteen dollars and fifty-one cents ;

To J. G. Rudisill, one hundred and nineteen dollars and twenty cents ;

To H. H. Rowland, twenty-one dollars ;

To W. H. Ghun, three dollars ;

To Jas. D. Wyan, seventy-two dollars and ten cents ;

To Joseph Commander, one hundred and sixty-seven dollars and sixty cents ;

To Snell & Haws, two hundred and eight dollars ;

To W. W. Ward, one hundred and thirty dollars ;

To Hazard Powd. Co., J. H. Hall, agt, one thousand nine hundred and five dollars and twenty-five cents ;

To Makepeace & McRae, twenty-four dollars ;

To J. S. McElroy, two hundred and thirty-two dollars and fifty-one cents ;

To J. C. Rudisill, twenty-six dollars and twenty-five cents ;

To W. H. Carrer, ass., one hundred and twenty-nine dollars and eighty-two cents ;

To Harnett county, three thousand seven hundred and eight dollars and fifty-three cents ;

To D. Pendar & Co., twenty-one dollars and fifty-two cents ;

To M. Witty, one hundred and twenty-six dollars ;

To D. C. Murray, forty-one dollars and forty cents ;

To Cobb & Neisbit, twenty-four dollars and forty-three cents ;

9

To Larry Newson, three hundred and seventy-five dollars;

To A. G. Carter, eleven dollars and seventy-five cents;

To Isaac House, seventeen dollars and ten cents;

To S. Satterwhite, fifty dollars;

To Jas. H. Holt, twenty-eight dollars and forty cents;

To J. B. Fulton, one hundred and thirty-seven dollars and forty cents;

To G. W. Goolake, sixty-six dollars and thirty-four cents;

To Summey, Speres & Co., one thousand two hundred and eight dollars and ninety-four cents;

To E. L. Triplett, thirty-six dollars and fifty cents;

To B. H. Merriman, fourteen dollars and eighty-seven cents;

To Jesse S. Smith, sixty-six dollars and sixty-five cents;

To B. J. Smith, twenty-two dollars;

To Thos. G. Whitaker, fourteen dollars;

To T. L. Skinner, and J. W. L. Benton, agt., six hundred and eight dollars;

To Green county, four thousand two hundred and forty dollars and seven cents;

To Perquimans county, six thousand nine hundred and six dollars and thirty-five cents;

To Catawba county, two thousand eight hundred and fifty-six dollars and sixty-one cents;

To Lincoln county, four thousand and seventy-six dollars and forty-three cents;

To Washington county, six thousand three hundred and twenty-six dollars and forty-three cents;

To Z. B. Vance, one thousand eight hundred and sixteen dollars and twenty-eight cents;

To H. T. Wolstenholmes, two hundred and eighty-six dollars and forty-five cents;

To P. H. Thrash, nine hundred and forty-four dollars and thirty cents;

To Committee of Safety at Newbern, H. T. Jenkins, assignee, four thousand five hundred and eighty-one dollars and eighty-six cents;

To Camden county, eight thousand five hundred and one dollars and ninety-seven cents;

To Union county, six thousand and ninety-one dollars and eighteen cents;

To Rowan county, two thousand six hundred and forty-five dollars and eighty-six cents;

To Jones county, five thousand three hundred and twenty dollars and ninety-seven cents;

To Moore county, five thousand four hundred and twenty-six dollars and six cents;

To Warren county, one thousand nine hundred and sixty-five dollars and ninety-eight cents;

To New Hanover county, seven thousand one hundred and seventy-two dollars and eighty-three cents;

To Robinson county, six thousand two hundred and twenty-five dollars and eight cents;

To Forsyth county, seven thousand five hundred and seventy-eight dollars and nineteen cents;

To Pasquotank county, eight thousand and fifty dollars and fourteen cents;

To Commissioners of the Town of Wilmington, fifty-eight thousand four hundred and forty-seven dollars and sixty cents;

To Sampson county, ten thousand six hundred and sixty-two dollars and thirty-nine cents;

To Chatham county, four thousand three hundred and forty dollars and forty-one cents;

To Davie county, four thousand eight hundred and twenty-six dollars and seventy-nine cents;

To Johnston county, seven thousand three hundred and seventy dollars and ninety-three cents;

To Guilford county, five thousand seven hundred and ninety-five dollars and ten cents;

To Randolph county, five thousand seven hundred and seventy-two dollars and sixty-three cents;

To Duplin county, three thousand seven hundred and ninety dollars and fifty-seven cents;

To Beaufort county, fourteen thousand six hundred and ninety-seven dollars and six cents;

Board of
Claims—
Disbursements.

To Charles H. K. Taylor, ass., five hundred and four dollars and sixty-eight cents ;

To R. L. Myres, agent for Newbern, Washington, and Hyde county Steamboat Company, three thousand dollars;

To Edwin Want, three hundred and ninety-nine dollars and sixty-five cents :

To Martin county, seven thousand two hundred and sixty-seven dollars and ninety-seven cents ;

To J. R. Bailey, four dollars and twenty cents ;

To C. E. Shober, trustee for W. J. McConnel, twenty-seven dollars and eighty cents ;

To Currituck county, six thousand one hundred and twenty-four dollars and five cents ;

To Yadkin county, five thousand four hundred and fifty-nine dollars and four cents ;

The foregoing sums having been allowed to the persons, counties, companies, &c., by the Board of Claims, and specified in the report of said Board made to this Convention at the present session.

[SIGNED,]   RICHARD H. SMITH,
                in behalf of Finance Committee.

December 11, 1861.

[*Ratified the* 12th *day of December*, 1861.]

[No. 18.] AN ORDINANCE TO REGULATE MILITIA MUSTER.

To assemble
once a month.

Be it ordained by this Convention, and it is hereby ordained by the authority of the same, That the militia of this State shall not be required to assemble for the purpose of drill and muster, more than once in each month, except for battalion or regimental muster. [*Ratified the 12th day of December,* 1861.]

AN ORDINANCE FOR SUPPRFSSING OPPRESSIVE [No. 19.]
SPECULATION UPON THE PRESENT NECESSI-
TIES OF THE PEOPLE.

1. *Be it ordained by the people of North Carolina, in* Makes specula-
Convention assembled, and it is hereby ordained by the tion a misdemeanor.
authority of the same, That whoever shall engross or get
into his hands by buying, contracting, or other means,
except by producing, corn or other grain growing in the
fields, or any other corn or grain, pork, or beef, either fish,
salted or smoked, cheese, fish, coffee, sugar, tea, salt, saltpetre, or other dead victuals whatever, and also leather, to
the intent to sell the same again at unreasonable prices, or
to keep the same from market, and prevent the same from
passing into the hands and use of the people, or to any
other intent than to his own use and consumption, or for
sale at reasonable prices, or for charitable distribution
amongst poor and necessitous persons : and, whosoever having in his hands, by the means aforesaid, any of the before-
mentioned articles not intended for his own use, or that of
his family or dependants, or for some such charitable use
as aforesaid, shall refuse to sell the same to, or shall ask
and demand therefor unreasonable prices, from any person
or persons desiring and offering to purchase for their own
personal use, or for that of their families or dependants, or
for such charitable use as aforesaid, shall be deemed an unlawful engrosser; and whosoever shall make any motion,
by word, letter, message, or otherwise, to any person or
persons, for the enhancing of the price, or dearer selling of
anything above mentioned, or else dissuade, move, or stir
any one coming, or purposing to come to any city, market,
post, or place within this State, to abstain, forbear to bring,
or convey any of the things before rehearsed to any such
city, town, market, or other place to be sold, shall be deemed
a forestaller; and whosover shall make any promise, enter
into any agreement, or come to any understanding with any
other person or persons, that he shall not sell any of the
things before rehearsed, but at certain prices, or at not less

than certain prices, shall be deemed an unlawful conspirator: and any person, upon conviction of either of the said offences, by verdict or confession, shall be punished as for a misdemeanor, and shall be required to enter into recognizance with sufficient surety for his good behavior for the space of three years, in such sums as the court may direct: *Provided,* That upon sufficient cause being shown, upon affidavit, the court shall have power to order the taking of depositions to be read in behalf of the accused, upon such terms as the court may decree on trial of cases arising under this ordinance.

2. *And be it further ordained,* That this ordinance shall be in force during the present war only, except as to prosecutions which may be pending and undetermined at the end of the war; and may, in the mean time, be repealed or modified by the General Assembly. [*Ratified the* 11th *day of December,* 1861.]

[No. 20.] AN ORDINANCE FOR CONTINUING THE BOARD CREATED BY AN ORDINANCE OF THIS CONVENTION, PASSED THE EIGHTH DAY OF JUNE, 1861, ENTITLED AN ORDINANCE TO PROVIDE FOR THE APPOINTMENT OF A BOARD OF CLAIMS, AND FOR ENLARGING THE POWERS AND DUTIES OF SAID BOARD.

1. *Be it ordained by this Convention, and it is hereby ordained by the authority of the same,* That the above-recited ordinance, and the Board thereby created, be, and the same are hereby continued and extended until the first day of January, which shall be in the year one thousand eight hundred and sixty-three, subject, however, to any provision hereafter made on the subject by this Convention, previous to the time mentioned.

2. *Be it further ordained,* That besides, and in addition to the duties conferred and enjoined by said ordinance, the said Board shall have power, and it shall be their duty to

examine and pass upon all accounts for expenditures made,
or responsibilities incurred, or allowances claimed by any
and every disbursing agent which have not already been
finally settled, and allowed at the Treasury, according to
existing law, and no such account shall hereafter be settled,
allowed, or paid at the Treasury, unless, and until the same
shall have first been passed upon and allowed and certified
by the said Board, and when, on the examination of any
such claim, or of any contract made, the Board shall be
satisfied that any disbursing officer or agent of the State,
shall have been guilty of any fraud, peculation, or other
malfeasance in his said office, or agency, or where any such
officer or agent shall fail to account for, and pay into
the Treasury, or unto the person or persons entitled to
receive the same, all such funds of the State, as in virtue of
his office or agency, he ought so to account for and pay over,
it shall be the duty of the Board to report the same to the
Governor, who shall, forthwith, dismiss the defaulting officer or agent from his said office or agency, and the Board
shall also notify the Attorney General thereof, whose duty
it shall be to bring suit for the recovery of all balances due,
and to institute proceedings, by way of indictment or otherwise, for the punishment of such officer or agent, and the
Superior Court of Law, or Court of Equity, for Wake
county, shall have jurisdiction of such proceedings according
to the nature thereof.

3. *Be it further ordained*, That for the making of a full
investigation of all cases under the second section of this
ordinance, for the discovery of any fraud, peculation or
other malfeasance, and for the ascertainment of the true
state of any account or claim, the Board shall have power
to compel the attendance of witnesses, the production of
papers, and to examine not only the witnesses, but any such
officer or agent, upon interrogations either verbal or written,
as the Board may deem proper, and to compel answer
thereto by process of contempt, as is usual in Courts of
Record of common law jurisdiction.

4. *Be it further ordained*, That all disbursing officers
and agents intrusted with the care and expenditure of the
funds of the State, whose accounts and dealings shall not
have been already finally settled according to existing laws,
shall make quarterly reports and exhibits of their dealings
and transactions therein to said Board, with the vouchers
belonging thereto, at such time in each quarter as the said
Board may appoint, by notice, to the said officer or agent,
in writing, and the said officer or agent so notified, shall
attend before said Board, from day to day, to give such
explanations, written or verbal, as the said Board may
require, and in all things, to submit to and comply with
such directions as the said Board may make, touching the
examining, auditing, and passing of such their accounts, and
if any such officer or agent shall neglect or refuse to perform anything made his duty in the premises, he shall be
reported by the Board to the Governor, who shall forthwith
dismiss such officer or agent from his said office or agency,
and the accounts or claims of such officer or agent shall not
be allowed, paid, or settled, but upon the certificate of the
said Board that the same are correct.

5. *Be it further ordained*, That it shall be the duty of
the said Board to make a semi-annual report to the Governor of the financial condition of the State, with such
recommendations and suggestions as they may think proper,
and the Governor shall lay the same before the Legislature.

6. *Be it further ordained*, That instead of the per diem
compensation allowed said Board by said ordinance of the
8th of June, 1861, each of the said Commissioners shall
be allowed a salary at the rate of two thousand dollars per
annum, payable quarterly, at the Treasury, and that the
said Board be, and they are hereby authorized to employ a
messenger at a cost not to exceed one dollar per day, to be
paid upon the certificate of the Board at the Treasury.

7. *Be it further ordained*, That it shall be the duty of
said Board to prepare the accounts of the disbursements of
North Carolina on account of the war, in such a way and

with such vouchers as shall enable the State to be hereafter reimbursed by the Confederate Government. [*Ratified the 11th day of December*, 1861.]

RESOLUTION CONCERNING POSTPONING THE [No. 21.] PUBLICATION OF COLONIAL RECORDS.

WHEREAS, Resolutions ratified the twenty-third of February, 1861, were passed at the last General Assembly, directing the printing of certain colonial and other records:

Resolved, That the publication of the same be suspended until further order from this Convention, or of the General Assembly of the State. [*Ratified the 12th day of December*, 1861.] <small>Suspends publication</small>

RESOLUTION AUTHORIZING THE PRESIDENT [No. 22.] TO CALL THIS CONVENTION TOGETHER IF THE PUBLIC INTEREST REQUIRE IT.

Resolved, That the President of this Convention, or in the event of his death, the committee named in the resolution of the last session, be empowered to convene this Convention before the twentieth of January next, if the public exigencies shall require it. [*Ratified the 13th day of December*, 1861.] <small>To convene the Convention before the 20th January, if necessary</small>

RESOLUTION IN FAVOR OF THE DOORKEEPER [No. 23.] AND ASSISTANT DOORKEEPERS.

Resolved, That the Doorkeeper and Assistant Doorkeepers to this Convention be allowed twenty-five dollars each for extra services at the present session, to be paid by the Treasurer out of any monies not otherwise appropriated. [*Ratified the 13th day of December*, 1861.] . <small>Allows $25 each extra</small>

10

[No. 24] AN ORDINANCE TO AUTHORIZE THE RAISING
OF A BATTALION OF SIX COMPANIES. OR
REGIMENT OF TROOPS FOR TWELVE MONTHS.

The Governor authorized to receive &c.

Be it ordained by this Convention, and it is hereby ordained by the authority of the same, That the Governor is authorized to receive into the service a Battalion of Infantry, to consist of six companies, for twelve months, or a regiment of ten companies, to be composed of volunteers who belonged to the First Regiment of North Carolina Volunteers, (the LaFayette Light Infantry, and the Independent Light Infantry of the town of Fayetteville included,) and such others as may enroll themselves with them.

Companies and Regiment to elect their commissioned officers.

Be it further ordained, That the said companies shall have the right to elect their commissioned officers, and the battalion shall have the right to elect a Lieutenant Colonel and a Major, and Colonel, if a regiment be formed, said officers of companies and of the battalion or regiment to be chosen in accordance with the law now in force, providing for the election of officers by the twelve months volunteers : *Provided, however,* That the said battalion or regiment shall be transferred within convenient time to, and accepted by the government of the Confederate States.
[*Ratified the* 12*th day of December,* 1861.]

[No. 25.] RESOLUTION TO PUBLISH THE ORDINANCES.

To be published in three newspapers

Resolved, That the Secretary of State have the Ordinances and Resolutions passed at this session of the Convention published in three newspapers printed in the city Raleigh, as soon as it can be conveniently done. [*Ratified the* 12*th day of December,* 1861.]

A RESOLUTION ASKING INFORMATION AS TO [No. 26.] THE STATE AND CONDITION OF THE CAPE FEAR AND DEEP RIVER IMPROVEMENT.

WHEREAS, In February last the General Assembly en- Preamble.
acted that the Board of Managers appointed to repair and
continue the improvement of the Cape Fear and Deep
River Improvement, and for this purpose placed at their
disposal thirty thousand dollars ; also authorized and required the Commissioners of the Cape Fear and Deep
River Navigation Company to sell as soon as they may
deem advisable the States' interest in said works, and
whereas, it is represented that said works are likely to suffer great damage from the want of repairs that would cost
but a small sum :

Resolved, That His Excellency, the Governor, be re- Information
spectfully requested to inform this Convention of the state asked of the
Governor.
and condition of said works, and all the information in his
possession as to what hath been done, or is likely to be
done under said act of Assembly.

Resolved, further, That said Board of Managers be Board of Mana-
requested to report at the earliest day convenient to this gers requested
to report.
Convention all that they have done under said act of Assembly, a full and detailed account of the state and condition of said improvement, and what in their judgment is
the best to be done with the same. [*Ratified the* 12th *day*
of December, 1861.]

RESOLUTION IN FAVOR OF D. D. FEREBEE, ESQ. [No. 27.]

Resolved, That the Treasurer pay to D. D. Ferebee, the Pays $38
amount of his expenses incurred as Commissioner to Richmond, amounting to thirty-eight dollars. [*Ratified the*
13th *day of December,* 1861.]

ORDINANCES AND RESOLUTIONS

PASSED BY

THE STATE CONVENTION

OF

NORTH CAROLINA.

'

𝔗𝔥𝔦𝔯𝔡 𝔖𝔢𝔰𝔰𝔦𝔬𝔫 𝔦𝔫 𝔍𝔞𝔫𝔲𝔞𝔯𝔶 𝔞𝔫𝔡 𝔉𝔢𝔟𝔯𝔲𝔞𝔯𝔶, 1862.

ORDINANCES AND RESOLUTIONS

OF THE

STATE CONVENTION

OF

NORTH CAROLINA.

THIRD SESSION IN JANUARY AND FEBRUARY, 1862.

AN ORDINANCE TO AUTHORIZE THE GOVERNOR TO EMBODY THE MILITIA FOR THE DEFENCE OF THE STATE. [No. 1.]

Be it ordained by the Delegates of the people of North Carolina, in Convention assembled, and it is hereby ordained by the authority of the same, That for the emergency mentioned in his message of to-day, the Governor of the State is hereby authorized to order out such portions of the militia, as he may deem necessary to repel the invasion of the State. [*Ratified the* 21st *day of January,* 1862.]

To expel Invasion

AN ORDINANCE TO MODIFY AND PERFECT AN ORDINANCE PASSED AT THE LAST SESSION OF THE CONVENTION, ENTITLED "AN ORDINANCE TO PROVIDE FOR THE RAISING OF MONEY FOR THE SUPPORT OF GOVERNMENT, AND FOR THE ISSUE OF TREASURY NOTES FOR THE PURPOSE OF PAYING THE PUBLIC DEBT AND PURCHASING SUPPLIES [No. 2.]

FOR THE MILITARY FORCES EMPLOYED FOR DEFENCE IN THE PRESENT WAR, AND FOR OTHER PURPOSES.

1. *Be it ordained by the Delegates of the people of North Carolina, in Convention assembled, and it is hereby ordained by th authority of the same,* That so much of the ordinance passed at the last session of this Convention, entitled "An Ordinance to provide for the raising of money for the support of Government, and for the issue of Treasury notes for the purpose of paying the public debt, and purchasing supplies for the military forces employed for defence in the present war, and for other purposes," as provides for the Treasury notes therein provided for, to bear interest from date, be rescinded and annulled: *Provided,* That this ordinance shall not operate on the notes issued before the passage of this ordinance.

2. *Be it further ordained,* That the said ordinance be so amended as to provide and require that [of] the whole of the Treasury notes hereafter to be issued under the provision of said ordinance, one-half shall be issued of the denominations of five dollars, one-fourth of the denominations of ten dollars, and the other fourth of the denominations of twenty dollars, and in the course of issuing the said notes, from time to time, the said relative proportions shall be observed as near as may be. [*Ratified the 25th day of January, 1862.*]

[No. 3.] ## A RESOLUTION AUTHORIZING WM. B. GULICK TO USE CENSUS RETURNS.

Resolved, That the Secretary of State be authorized to allow Wm. B. Gulick to use, either in or out of his office, for two months, the Census Returns of 1860, or until they had be called for by an authorized agent of the Government of the Confederate States, provided the same be not removed from the City of Raleigh. [*Ratified the 25th day of January, 1862.*]

AN ORDINANCE TO RATIFY AND CONFIRM [No. 4.] THE ACTS AND JUDICIAL PROCEEDINGS OF THE SUPERIOR COURTS LATELY HELD BY HIS HONOR, JUDGE FRENCH, IN THE COUNTIES OF HENDERSON, BUNCOMBE, MADISON AND YANCEY.

WHEREAS, The Superior Courts for the counties of Hen- *Courts held at the wrong times* derson, Buncombe, Madison and Yancey, at the Fall Terms thereof were, by mistake, held at the wrong time; and, *whereas*, pleas were filed, judgments rendered, recognizances entered into, judgments found, and various other acts were done by said courts:

1. *Be it ordained by the Delegates of the people of North* *Proceedings of the Courts ratified.* *Carolina, in Convention assembled, and it is hereby ordained by the authority of the same,* That the said pleas, judgments, recognizances, indictments, and all other judicial proceedings, which were rendered, entered and found at the terms of the courts aforesaid, are hereby made valid, and in all things ratified and confirmed.

2. *Be it further ordained,* That the Courts of Pleas *Times of holding the Courts specified.* and Quarter Sessions to be held hereafter for the counties of Henderson, Buncombe, Madison, Yancey and Polk, at the Fall Terms, be held at the following times, viz: Henderson, on the second Monday after the fourth Monday in September; Buncombe, on the third Monday after the fourth Monday in September; Madison, on the fourth Monday after the fourth Monday in September; Yancey, on the fifth Monday after the fourth Monday in September; and Polk on the twelfth Monday after the fourth Monday in September in each and every year. This section to continue in force until the same may be repealed by act of the Legislature or otherwise. [*Ratified the 27th day of January*, 1862.]

11

[No. 5.] AN ORDINANCE TO ABROGATE THE FOURTH
          SECTION OF AN ACT OF THE LEGISLATURE
          OF THE STATE OF NORTH CAROLINA, PASSED
          AT THE LAST EXTRA SESSION, ENTITLED,
          "AN ACT ENTITLED REVENUE."

Abrogated the fourth section   *Be it ordained by the Delegates of the people of North
Carolina in Convention assembled, and it is hereby ordained
by the authority of the same,* That the fourth section of an
act of the last extra session of the General Assembly of
the State of North Carolina, entitled "An Act entitled
Revenue," be, and the same is hereby annulled and abrogated. [*Ratified the 30th day of January,* 1862.]

———————————

[No. 6.] AN ODINANCE TO ENCOURAGE THE MINING
          AND MANUFACTURING OF SALT IN THE IN-
          TERIOR OF THIS STATE.

*The Chatham
Salt Mining
and Manufactu-
rers' Company.*   WHEREAS, It is of great importance to manufacture
Salt in the interior of this State ; and whereas, a company
has been incorporated under the name and style of "The
Chatham Salt Mining and Manufacturing Company,"
which is operating for that purpose in the county of Chatham ; therefore,

*Exempt officers
from militia
duty*   1. *Be it ordained by the Delegates of the people of North
Carolina in Convention assembled, and it is hereby ordained
by the authority of the same,* That the President and oper-
atives of said company, to the number of six, be, and they
are hereby exempted from militia duty, for the space of
six months, except in case of invasion, insurrection, or
upon a requisition for troops by the President of the Confederate States.

Capital stock   2. *Be it further ordained,* That said Company may increase its capital stock to an amount not exceeding ten
thousand dollars.

*Exempt from
taxation*   3. *Be it further ordained,* That the capital stock of said
Company be exempted from taxation for six months. [*Ratified the 30th day of January,* 1862.]

AN ORDINANCE IN ADDITION TO AND AMEND- [No. 7.]
MENT OF AN ACT OF THE GENERAL ASSEM-
BLY, RATIFIED THE 15TH DAY OF FEBRUARY,
1861, ENTITLED "AN ACT TO INCORPORATE
THE CHATHAM RAILROAD COMPANY," AND
TO REPEAL AN ACT SUPPLEMENTAL THERE-
TO, RATIFIED THE 23RD DAY OF FEBRUARY,
1861.

1. *Be it ordained by the Delegates of the people of North* To connect with the N. C. R. R.
Carolina in Convention assembled, and it is hereby ordained at or within 12
by the authority of the same, That section first of an act of miles of Raleigh
the General Assembly, ratified the fifteenth day of Febru-
ary, one thousand eight hundred and sixty-one, entitled
"An Act incorporating the Chatham Railroad Company,"
be amended by inserting after the words, "from the Coalfields, in the county of Chatham, through said county,"
the words, connect with the North Carolina Railroad at, so
as to make the section read, "to connect with the North
Carolina Railroad at Raleigh, or some point west of Raleigh
not exceeding twelve miles."

2. *Be it further ordained,* That the proviso in section Provision
four of said act of the General Assembly be stricken out. stricken out

3. *Be it further ordained,* That an act of the General Repeals supple-
Assembly, ratified on the twenty-third day of February, mental act.
one thousand eight hundred and sixty-one, entitled "An
Act supplemental to an act passed at the present session
of the General Assembly, entitled "An Act to incorporate
the Chatham Railroad Company," be, and the same is hereby repealed and abrogated.

4. *Be it further ordained,* That all such solvent corpo- other corpora-
rations as may or shall subscribe to the capital stock of the ing to the
said Chatham Railroad Company, may make their bonds capital stock of
payable to the Public Treasurer of the State of North Company
Carolina for the amount of their subscriptions to said capital stock, and no more; which said bonds are to be signed
by the Presidents, and under the seals respectively of said
corporations, and made for any sums not under five hun-

dred dollars each, to bear interest at the rate of six per
cent. per annum, which interest is to be paid semi-annually,
to-wit: the first Monday in January and July in each and
every year; and the principal of said bonds to be made
payable twenty years after date; and these bonds, so
authorized to be made, may be deposited with the Public
Treasurer of the State, who shall then issue and deliver to
the several corporations so subscribing and depositing their
bonds as aforesaid, the coupon bonds of the State of North
Carolina, to the amount of their subscriptions respectively,
and made for the sums of five hundred dollars and one
thousand dollars, to bear interest at the rate of six per
cent. per annum, which interest is to be paid semi-annually,
on the first Monday in January and July in each and every
year, and the principal of said bonds to be made payable
twenty years after date: *Provided*, That said bonds shall
not exceed, in the aggregate, the sum of eight hundred
thousand dollars; and *Provided, also*, That said Chatham
Railroad Company shall execute and deliver to the Governor of the State of North Carolina a deed of mortgage
under the seal of said Company, wherein and whereby
shall be conveyed to the Governor and his successors in
office, for the use and benefit of the State, all the estate,
both real and personal, belonging to said Company, or in
any manner pertaining to the same, conditioned for indem-
nifying and saving harmless the State of North Carolina
from the payment of the whole or any part of the bonds
of the State, authorized by this ordinance to be made by
the Public Treasurer, and delivered to the several corporations subscribing as aforesaid to the capital stock of said
Chatham Railroad Company. In addition to the deed of
mortgage, hereinbefore required to be executed and delivered by the Chatham Railroad Company, the State of
North Carolina shall, by this ordinance, have a lein upon
the estate, both real and personal, of said company, which
they may now have or may hereafter acquire, to secure the
principal and interest of the bonds of this State authorized to be issued as aforesaid.

5. *Be it further ordained*, That said bonds of the State, so made by the Public Treasurer, shall be received by the said Chatham Railroad Company in payment of subscriptions made as aforesaid by such corporations to the capital stock of said Chatham Railroad Company.

Bonds of the State to be received by the Company.

6. *Be it further ordained*, That said corporations so subscribing and depositing their bonds as aforesaid with the Treasurer of the State, shall be allowed to redeem their bonds at any time before maturity, in the currency of the State, on giving thirty days notice to the Treasurer of this State of their intention so to do.

Corporations allowed to redeem their bonds.

7. *Be it further ordained*, That the said Railroad may be constructed with termini at any point or points in the said Coalfields region that the stockholders in said Company may agree upon with the approbation of the Board of Internal Improvements.

Termini.

8. *Be it further ordained*, That the corporate authorities of incorporated towns subscribing to the capital stock of said Chatham Railroad Company, in order to provide for the payment of their subscriptions, and of the principal and interest of bonds for that purpose, by them issued, shall have authority to lay and collect taxes from all subjects, which, under the charters of said towns, are taxable.

Incorporated towns to lay a tax to pay their subscriptions.

9. *Be it further ordained*, That the solvency of such corporations as may desire to subscribe to the capital stock of said Chatham Railroad Company shall be judged of by the Board of Internal Improvements.

Solvency.

10. *Be it further ordained*, That all laws and parts of laws, all acts or parts of acts inconsistent with the provissons of this ordinance, are hereby repealed and abrogated.

[*Ratified the 30th day of January, 1862.*]

AN ORDINANCE TO INCORPORATE THE PIEDMONT RAILROAD COMPANY.   [No. 8.]

1. *Be it ordained by the Delegates of the people of North Carolina, in Convention assembled, and it is hereby ordained by the authority of the same,* That a company by the name

Capital stock $1,600,000.

and style of the "Piedmont Railroad Company," be, and the same is hereby incorporated, with a capital stock of fifteen hundred thousand dollars, divided into shares of one hundred dollars each, for the purpose of constructing a railroad on the best, cheapest, most direct and practicable route from the Richmond and Danville Railroad to the North Carolina Railroad.

2. *Be it further ordained*, That for the purpose of creating the capital stock of said company, the following persons be, and they are hereby appointed general commissioners: Wm. T. Sutherlin, of Danville; William P. Watt, John H. Dillard, George D. Boyd and William B. Carter, of Rockingham; Phil. Barrow, John F. Poindexter and A. J. Stafford, of Forsyth county; William A. Lash, John J. Martin and Jas. Riason, of Stokes county: Jesse H. Lindsay, Levi M. Scott and Ralph Görrell, of Guilford county: Bedford Brown, Thomas D. Johnston, Allen Green and Montford McGee, of Caswell county; Giles Mebane, Jesse Gant and Eli F. Watson, of Alamance; Jno. W. Cunningham, Edwin G. Read and Thos. McGee, of the county of Person; Wm. Johnston, of the town of Charlotte; James C. Turrentine and Wm. F. Strayhorn, of the county of Orange; Benjamin A. Kittrell, of the town of Lexington; H. C. Jones, Sr., of Salisbury; Jonathan Worth, of the town of Ashboro'; Wm. P. Taylor, of Pittsboro'; whose duty it shall be to direct the opening of books for subscriptions of stock at such times and places, and under such persons as they, or a majority of them, may deem proper, and in the mean time it shall and may be lawful for books of subscriptions to said stock to be opened in the town of Charlotte under the direction of John A. Young, Wm. Johnston and James W. Osborne, or any one of them: in Concord, under the direction of V. M. Barringer, Caleb Phifer and Daniel Coleman, or any one of them: in Salisbury, under the direction of Nathaniel Boyden, N. N. Fleming, J. I. Shaver, or any one of them; at Lexington, under the direction of Wm. R. Holt, John P. Mabrey and Samuel Hargrove, or any one of them: at

High Point, under the direction of W. F. Bowman, Dr. Robert Lindsay and Nathan Hunt, or any one of them; at Greensboro', under the direction of James Sloan, Jed. H. Lindsay and J. A. Long, or any one of them; at Salem, under the direction of D. H. Starbuck, J. G. Lash, Francis Fries and C. L. Bonner, or any one of them; at Danbury, under the direction of Nathaniel Moody, A. H. Joyce and S. Taylor, or any one of them; at Graham, under the direction of Thomas Ruffin, Jr., John Trollinger and Edward Holt, or any one of them; at Roxboro', under the direction of Charles Winstead, Dr. C. H. Jordan and Green Williams, or any one of them; at Yanceyville, under the direction of John Kerr, Dr. N. M. Roan and Thomas W. Graves, or any one of them; at Milton, under the direction of Samuel Watkins, John Wilson and Thomas Donaho, or any one of them; at Wentworth, under the direction of John W. Ellington, W. M. Ellington and B. J. Low, or any one of them; at Madson, under the direction of Wm. L. Scales, Joseph H. Cardwell and Nicholas Dalton, or any one of them; at Leaksville, under the direction of George L. Aiken, Jones W. Burton and E. T. Brodnax, or any one of them; at High Rock, under the direction of Francis L. Simpson, Dr. R. H. Scales and Geo. W. Garret, or any one of them; at Danville, Va., under the direction of William T. Sutherlin, James M. Williams and Dr. T. P. Atkinson, or any one of them; at Hillsboro', under the direction of J. C. Turrentine, Henry K. Nash and W. F. Strayhorn, or any one them; and in the city of Richmond, Va., under the direction of A. Y. Stokes, Lewis E. Harvey and Thomas N. Brockenbrough, or any one of them; and said commissioners shall have power to appoint a Chairman of their body, Treasurer, and all other officers their organization may require, and sue for and recover all sums of money that ought, under this ordinance, to be recovered by them in the name of said corporation.

3. *Be it further ordained,* That all persons who are, by Subscriptions. this ordinance authorized, or who may be hereafter, by the

general commissioners, authorized to open books of sub-scription, may do so at any time after the passage of this ordinance, upon giving twenty days notice of the time and place when said books shall be opened, and said books shall be kept open for the space of thirty days, at least, and as long thereafter as the general commissioners shall direct ; and that all subscriptions of stock shall be in shares of hundred dollars, the subscriber paying, at the time he makes his subscription, five dollars on each share by him subscribed, to the person or persons authorized to receive such subscriptions ; and upon closing the books, all such sums as shall have thus been received of subscribers, on the first cash instalment, shall be paid over to the general commissioners, by the persons receiving the same, and in case of failure to pay, as aforesaid, such person or persons, receiving said money, shall be personally liable to said general commissioners, before the organization of said company, and to the company itself, after the organization, to be recovered within the Superior Courts of Law within this State, in the county where such delinquent resides, or if he resides in another State, then, in any court in such State having competent jurisdiction. The general commissioners shall have power to call on and require all persons empowered to receive subscriptions of stock, at any time, and from time to time, as a majority of them may think proper, to make return of the stock by them respectively received, and to make payment of all sums of money paid by subscribers ; that all persons receiving subscriptions of stock shall pass a receipt to the subscriber or subscribers for the payment of the first instalment, as heretofore required to be paid, and upon their settlement with the general commissioners as aforesaid, it shall be the duty of said general commissioners, in like manner, to pass their receipts for all sums thus received to the persons from whom received, and such receipts shall be taken and held to be good and sufficient vouchers to persons holding them ; that subscriptions of stock may be received as aforesaid or as hereafter provided for, to the amount of fifteen hundred thousand dollars.

4. *Be it further ordained,* That it shall be the duty of The Company to be declared a corporate body when $100,000 is subscribed. said general commissioners to direct and authorize said books of subscription to be kept open until the sum of one hundred thousand dollars, at least, shall be subscribed in the manner aforesaid, and as soon as the said sum of one hundred thousand dollars, or upwards, shall be subscribed in manner aforesaid, and the sum of five dollars on each share paid as aforesaid, the subscribers to said stock shall be, and they are hereby declared to be a body politic, and corporate in fact and in law, by the name and style of the "Piedmont Railroad Company," with all the corporate powers and authority thereby created and granted, to be held and exercised by said company and their successors and assigns, in perpetuity, and by that name shall be capable, in law and in equity, to purchase, hold, lease, rent, sell or convey estates, real and personal, and to acquire the same by gift, devise or otherwise, so far as shall be necessary for the purposes embraced within the scope, object and intent of this charter, and shall have perpetual succession and a common seal, which [they] may use, alter or renew at pleasure, and by their corporate name, may sue and be sued, plead and be impleaded, in any court of law in this State or any other State; and shall have, posess and enjoy, all rights, privileges and immunities which railroad corporate bodies may and of right do exercise, and may make such by-laws, rules and regulations as are necessary for the government of the corporation, or for effecting the object for which it is created, not inconsistent with the laws of this State or of the Confederate States of America.

5. *Be it further ordained,* That as soon as the sum of Meeting of general commissioners. one hundred thousand dollars or upwards shall be subscribed, as aforesaid, it shall be the duty of the general commissioners to appoint a time for the stockholders to meet in the town of Greensboro', in the county of Guilford, which they shall cause to be previously published for the space of thirty days, in one or more newspapers; at which time and place, the said stockholders shall, in person or by proxy, proceed to elect, by ballot, nine Directors of the com-

12

pany, and to enact all such regulations and by-laws as may
be necessary for the government of said corporation, and
the transaction of its business. The persons elected directors at this meeting shall serve such period, not exceeding
one year, as the stockholders may direct; and at this meeting, the stockholders shall fix on a day and place or places
when and where the subsequent election of directors shall
be held, and such·elections shall thenceforth be annually
made; but if the day of annual elections should pass
without any election of directors, the corporation shall not
thereby be dissolved; but the directors in office shall so
remain until others are appointed, and it shall be lawful
on any other day to make and hold such elections in such
manner as may be prescribed by a by-law of the corporation.

6. *Be it further ordained,* That the affairs of said company shall be managed by a general board, to consist of
nine directors, to be elected by the stockholders from
among themselves, at their first and subsequent general
annual meetings, and no stockholder shall be elected a
director, nor serve as such, unless he be at the time of his
election the owner of five shares of stock, and shall continue to hold the same during the term of his service as
director.

7. *Be it further ordained,* That the President of said
company shall be chosen by ballot by a majority of the
directors from among themselves, with a salary to be fixed
by the stockholders in general meeting.

8. *Be it further ordained,* That all stockholders, not
being aliens, shall be entitled to vote either in person or
by proxy, the proxy being a stockholder, at all general
meetings, and the vote to which each stockholder shall be
entitled, shall be according to the number of shares he
may hold, as hereinafter provided.

9. *Be it further ordained,* That at the first general meeting of the stockholders, under this ordinance, a majority
all of the shares subscribed shall be represented before
proceeding to business; and if a sufficient number do not

appear on the day appointed, those who do attend shall have power to adjourn, from time to time, until a regular meeting be thus formed, and at such meeting the stockholders may provide by a by-law as to the number of stockholders, and the amount of stock to be held by them, which shall constitute a quorum for the transaction of business at all subsequent meetings.

10. *Be it further ordained*, That the general commissioners shall make their return of shares of stock subscribed for, at the first general meeting of the stockholders, and pay over to the directors elected at that meeting, or their authorized agent, all sums of money received from subscribers; and on failure to do so, they shall be personally liable to said company, to be recovered in like manner as other debts due the company.

11. *Be it further ordained*, That the Board of Directors may fill all vacancies which may occur in it during the period for which they have been elected, and in the absence of the President, may fill his place by electing a President *pro tem.* from among their number.

12. *Be it further ordained*, That said Board of Directors shall have power and authority to open books for further subscriptions to the stock of said company at such times and under such persons as they may designate, in the event the whole stock be not subscribed before the first general meeting of the stockholders, and to open and keep open such books, from time to time, until the whole amount of capital stock be subscribed.

13. *Be it further ordained*, That said company shall have power and proceed to construct, as speedily as possible, a railroad, with one or more tracks, from the North Carolina Railroad to the Richmond and Danville Railroad in Virginia, to be used and operated by steam power; and to the end that the said corporation may have power and authority to construct said road within the limits of the State of Virginia—this charter shall be transmitted by the President of this Convention to the Governor of Virginia, to the end that the legislative sanction of that State.

approving the ordinance, may be given to said company, to construct the railroad as aforesaid within the limits of that State: *Provided*, That the company formed under this charter shall have no power to discriminate, on either freight or travel, against the North Carolina Railroad, or roads in North Carolina connected with it.

Charter

14. *Be it further ordained*, That said company shall have the exclusive right of conveyance or transportation of persons, goods, merchandise and produce, over the road constructed by them, at such charges as may be fixed upon by a majority of the directors; and the said company may farm out their rights of transportation over their said railroad, subject to the rules above mentioned; and said company, and every person who may have received from them the right of transportation of goods, wares, and produce on said road, shall be deemed and taken to be a common carrier, as respects everything entrusted to them or him for transportation.

Instalment upon subscriptions

15. *Be it further ordained*, That the Board of Directors may call for the payment of the sums subscribed as stock in said company in such instalments as the interest of the said company may require; the call for each payment shall be published in one or more papers in this State for two months before the day of payment, and on failure of any stockholder to pay each instalment as thus required, the directors may sell at public auction, on a previous notice of ten days, for cash, all the stock subscribed for in said company by such stockholders, and convey the same to the purchaser at said sale, discharged from further liabilities; and if said sale of stock does not produce a sum sufficient to pay off the incidental expenses of sale, and the entire amount owing by such stockholder to the company for such subscription of stock, then, and in that case the whole of such balance shall be held and taken as due at once to the company, and may be recovered of such stockholder or his executors, administrators or assigns, at suit of said company, either by summary motion in any court of supreme jurisdiction in the county where the delinquent resides, on a

previous notice of ten days to said subscribers, or by action
of assumpsit in any court of competent jurisdiction, or by
warrant before a Justice of the Peace when the sum does
not exceed one hundred dollars; and in all cases of assignment of stock before the whole amount has been paid to
the company, then, for all sums due on such stock, both
the original subscribers and the first and all the subsequent
assignees shall be held liable to the company, and the same
may be recovered as above described.

16. *Be it further ordained,* That said company shall
issue certificates of stock to its members, and said stock
may be transferred in such manner and form as may be
directed by the by-laws of the company.

Certificates of stock.

17. *Be it further ordained,* That the debt of the stockholders due to the company for stock therein, either original proprietor, or as first or subsequent assignee, shall be
considered with equal dignity with judgments in the distribution of the assets of a deceased stockholder by his legal
representatives.

Debts of stock-holders to the Company.

18. *Be it further ordained,* That the Board of Directors
shall, once a year, at least, make a full report on the state
of the company and its affairs, to a general meeting of the
stockholders, and oftener if required by a by-law, and shall
have power to call a general meeting of the stockholders
when the board may deem expedient; and the company may
provide, in their by-laws, for occasional meetings being
called, and prescribe the mode thereof.

Board of Direc-tors to report to Stockholders.

19. *Be it further ordained,* That the said company may
purchase, have and hold, in fee or for a term of years, any
lands, tenements, or hereditaments which may be necessary
for said road, or appurtenances thereof, or for the erection
of depositories. store houses, houses for the officers, servants, or agents of the company, or for the workshops or
foundries to be used for said company, or for procuring
stone or other materials necessary to the construction of
the road, or for effecting transportation thereon.

Rights of Com-pany to pur-chase real estate.

20. *Be it further ordained,* That the company shall have
the right, when necessary, to conduct the said road across

Rights of the Company in running the road.

or along any public road or water course : *Provided*, That the said company shall not obstruct any public road without constructing another equally as good and convenient.

21. *Be it further ordained*, That when any land or right of way may be required by said company for the purpose of constructing their road, and for want of agreement as to the value thereof, or for any other cause, the same can not be purchased from the owner or owners—the same may be taken at a valuation to be made by five freeholders, selected by the County Court in the county where the right of way is situated : *Provided, nevertheless*, That if any person or persons over whose lands the road may pass, or if said company should be dissatisfied with the valuation of said freeholders, then, and in that case, the party so dissatisfied may have an appeal to the Superior Court in the county where the damage is done, or in either county where the land may lie, under the same rules, regulations and restrictions as in other classes of appeal ; the proceeding of the said freeholders, accompanied with a full description of said land or right of way, shall be returned under the hands and seals of a majority of them to the court from which the order was made, there to remain a matter of record ; and the lands or right of way so valued, shall vest in the said company so long as the same may be used for purposes of said Railroad, as soon as the valuation shall have been made, or when refused, may have been tendered : *Provided*, That on application for the appointment of freeholders under this section, it shall be made to appear to the satisfaction of the court, that at least ten days' previous notice has been given by the applicant to the owner or owners of the land proposed to be condemned, or if the owner or owners be infants or *non compos mentis*, then to the guardian or guardians of such owner or owners, if such guardian can be found within the county, or if he cannot be found, then such appointment shall not be made unless notice of the application shall 'have been published at least one month next preceding in some newspaper printed as conveniently as may be to the

court house of the county, and shall have been posted at
the door of the court house on the first day of the term of
said court to which the application is made: *Provided,
further,* That the valuation provided for in this section
shall be made on oath by the freeholders aforesaid, which
oath, any Justice of the Peace, or clerk, is authorized to
administer: *Provided, further,* That the right of condemnation herein granted, shall not authorize the said
company to invade the dwelling house, yard, garden or
burial ground of any individual without his consent.

22. *Be it further ordained,* That the right of said company to condemn lands in the manner as aforesaid, shall
extend to the condemning one hundred feet on each side
of the track of the road, measuring from the centre of the
same, unless in case of deep cuts and fillings, when said
company shall have power to condemn as much in addition
thereto as may be necessary for the purpose of constructing said road, and the company shall also have power to
condemn and appropriate lands in like manner for the constructing and building of depots, shops, warehouses, buildings for servants, agents, and persons employed on the
road, not exceeding four acres to any one lot or station.

Amount of land to be condemned.

23. *Be it further ordained,* That in the absence of any
contract or contracts with said company in relation to the
lands through which the said road may pass, signed by the
owner thereof, or his agent, or any claimant or person in
possession thereof, it shall be presumed that the land upon
which the said road may be constructed, together with the
space of one hundred feet on each side of the centre of
said road, has been granted to the said company by the
owner thereof, and the said company shall have good right
and title thereto, and shall have, hold and enjoy the same
as long as the same be used for the purposes of the road,
and no longer, unless the person or persons owning the
said land at the time that part of the said road which may
be on the said land was finished, or those claiming under
him, her or them, shall apply for an assignment of the
value of said lands, as hereinbefore directed, within two

Powers and privileges in regard to un-claimed lands

years next after that part of the said road which may be on said lands was finished; and in case the owner, or those claiming under him, her or them, shall not apply within two years next after the said part was finished, he, she or they shall be forever barred from recovering said land, or having any assessment or compensation therefor: *Provided*, Nothing herein contained shall affect the rights of *feme coverts*, or infants, until two years after the removal of their respective disabilities.

Vesting title to land.

24. *Be it further ordained.* That all lands not heretofore granted to any person within one hundred feet of the centre of said road, shall vest in the company so soon as the line of the road is definitely laid out through it, and any grant of said land shall thereafter be void.

Punishment for intrusion upon the road.

25. *Be it further ordained.* That if any person or persons shall intrude upon said railroad, by any manner of use thereof, or of the right and privilege connected therewith, without the permission, or contrary to the will of said company, he, she or they may be indicted for a misdemeanor, and upon conviction, fined and imprisoned by any court of competent jurisdiction.

Punishment for wanton damage to the road or any property of the company.

26. *Be it further ordained,* That if any person or persons shall willfully and maliciously destroy, or in any manner hurt or damage, or shall willfully and maliciously cause, or aid, or assist, or counsel and advise any other person or persons to destroy, or in any manner to hurt, damage, injure or obstruct the said railroad, or any bridge or vehicle used for or in the transportation thereon, any watertank, warehouse, or other property of said company, such person or persons, so offending, shall be liable to be indicted therefor, and on conviction, shall be imprisoned not less than one nor more than six months, and pay a fine, not exceeding five hundred dollars, nor less than twenty dollars, at the discretion of the court before which said conviction shall take place, and shall be further liable to pay all expenses for repairing the same: and it shall not be competent for any one so offending against the provisions of this clause to defend himself by pleading or giving

in evidence that he was the owner, agent, or servant of the
owner of the land where such destruction, hurt, damage.
injury or obstruction was done at the time the same was
done or caused to be done.

27. *Be it further ordained,* That every obstruction to Obstructions.
the safe and free passage of vehicles on said road shall be
deemed a public nuisance, and be abated as such by any
officer, agent or servant of said company, and the person
causing such obstruction may be indicted for erecting a
public nuisance.

28. *Be it further ordained,* That the said company shall Privileges of
transportation.
have the right to take at the storehouses they may estab- &c.
lish, or annex to their railroad, all goods, wares, merchandise, and produce intended for transportation, to prescribe
the rules of priority, and charge and receive such just and
reasonable compensation for storage as they, by rules, may
establish (which they shall cause to be published) as may
be fixed by agreement with the owners, which may be distinct from rates of transportation: *Provided,* That the said
company shall not charge nor receive storage on goods,
wares, merchandise or produce which may be delivered to
them at their regular depositories for immediate transportation, and which the company may have the power to
transport immediately.

29. *Be it further ordained,* That the profits of the Profit.
company, or so much thereof as the General Board may
deem advisable, shall, when the affairs of the company will
permit, be semi-annually divided among the stockholders
in proportion to the stock each may own.

30. *Be it further ordained,* That the following officers Officers and em
ployees exempt
and servants and persons in the actual employment of said from jury and
militia duty
company be, and they are hereby exempt from the performance of jury and ordinary militia duty: The President and Treasurer, the Board of Directors, Chief and
Assistant Engineers, the Secretary and Accountant of the
company, keepers of the depositories, guards stationed on
the road and at the bridges, and such persons as may be
working the locomotive engines and traveling with the cars

13

for the purpose of attending to the transport of produce, goods and passengers on the road.

be it

31. *Be it further ordained.* That if the Legislature of Virginia shall sanction this charter, and authorize the construction of said road within the limits of Virginia to the Richmond and Danville Railroad, and said road shall be so constructed, the said corporation hereby created shall, nevertheless, have power and authority to construct and build one or more branches of said road to the Coalfields of Dan River, and the navigable waters on Smith's river, in the county of Rockingham, and are hereby vested with the rights, powers, privileges and immunities to build and construct said branch or branches with which they are invested to build the main road; and the said road, with its branches, authorized to be constructed under this charter, shall be of the same guage as the North Carolina Railroad; and the North Carolina Railroad Company shall have the right, under this charter, to construct a branch of their road from Hillsboro' at [to] or near Danville.

Powers of the company

32. *Be it further ordained.* That for the purpose of ascertaining the best route for said road and its branches, and to locate the same, it shall be lawful for said company, by its engineers, servants and agents, to enter upon, examine and survey any land or lands that they may wish to examine for such purpose, free from any liability whatever.

Confederate States authorized to take the stock in the company.

33. *Be it further ordained,* That any one or more of the solvent incorporate railroad companies of the said States, and also the Confederate States of America, may subscribe for stock in said company, and should the Confederate States of America subscribe for and take the whole of such stock, or the larger part thereof, power and authority are given to said Confederate States of America to appoint for the time being the whole of the said Directors, anything in this ordinance to the contrary notwithstanding, and at once locate and commence the construction of said road, and hold the stock so taken by them until individuals and corporations shall be prepared to receive an assignment

of the same, or any part or parts thereof, as hereinafter provided.

34. *Be it further ordained,* That as soon as, under the supervision of the general commissioners, as by this ordinance provided, there shall be subscribed by the Confederate States of America, incorporated companies, or solvent individuals, not less than one hundred thousand dollars of stock, with the five per cent. thereon paid in, the same shall be certified by said general commissioners to said Directors, on which being done, it shall be the duty of said Directors to have the names of such stockholders recorded on the books of said company, together with the stock subscribed by each, and to cause to have issued to said stockholders certificates of stock in said company, (to each in proportion to the subscriptions made by them,) when they shall have paid up their subscriptions in full, including in their payments the five per cent. which they shall have paid to the said general commissioners, and which the said general commissioners, as hereinbefore provided, shall pay to said company.

Duties of general commissioners, directors, &c.

35. *Be it further ordained,* That as soon as subscribers other than the Confederate States of America, as herein provided, shall have their names as stockholders recorded on the books of said company as owners of not less than one hundred thousand dollars of stock, with the five per cent. thereon paid in, from and after that time such stockholders, in all general meetings, shall have power to elect five of the said nine Directors, and the President of the Confederate States of America, or such other person as the Confederate States may determine, to appoint four of said Directors, and continue to do so until the stock of the said Confederate States, by sale or transfer, shall be reduced to less than half of the entire stock of said company ; then, and from and after that time, the vote of the said Confederate States of America in the election of Directors, and on all other questions, shall be in proportion to the stock held by them : *Provided,* That at such elections no stockholder shall give more than two hundred votes.

The appointment of directors.

State reserves
the right to
connect any
other road with
this one.

36. *Be it further ordained,* That full right and privilege is hereby reserved to the State, or to any company hereafter to be incorporated under the authority of this State, to connect with the road hereby provided for, any other railroad leading therefrom to any part or parts of this State: *Provided,* That in joining such connection, no injury shall be done to the works of the company hereby incorporated.

Charter to
expire at the
end of 99 years.

37. *Be it further ordained,* That the corporate franchises and privileges hereby granted shall cease and determine at the expiration of ninety-nine years from the day of the passage of this ordinance. [*Ratified the 8th day of February,* 1862.]

[No. 9.] AN ORDINANCE TO INCORPORATE THE WASHINGTON AND TARBORO' RAILROAD COMPANY.

Capital stock
$400,000.

1. *Be it ordained by the Delegates of the people of North Carolina, in Convention assembled, and it is hereby ordained by the authority of the same,* That for the purpose of effecting a railroad communication between the town of Washington and the town of Tarboro', the formation of a corporate company, with a capital of four hundred thousand dollars. is hereby authorized, to be called the Washington and Tarboro' Railroad Company, and when formed in compliance with the conditions hereinafter prescribed, to have a corporate existence as a body politic in perpetuity.

Route of the
road.

2. *Be it further ordained,* That the said company be, and the same is hereby authorized to construct a railroad from the town of Washington, in the county of Beaufort, through the counties of Pitt and Edgecombe, to the town of Tarboro'.

Commissioners
to open books of
subscription.

3. *Be it further ordained,* That for the purpose of raising the capital stock of said company, it shall be lawful to open books under the direction of the following named commissioners, to-wit: At Washington, under the direction

of John Myers, Jos. Potts, Benj. F. Havens, B. M. Selby
and George H. Brown; at Pactolus, under the direction of
Churchill Perkins, Peyton A. Atkinson, J. G. B. Grimes,
Rippon Ward, and Henry Stancil; at Tarboro', under the
direction of John S. Dancy, R. H. Pender, R. R. Bridgers,
William S. Battle, and James R. Thigpen, and at such other
places and under the direction of such other persons as a
majority of the commissioners first named may deem proper,
for the purpose of receiving subscriptions to the amount of
four hundred thousand dollars, in shares of fifty dollars
each.

4. *Be it further ordained*, That the commissioners above
named, and all other persons who may hereafter be authorized as aforesaid to open books for subscriptions, shall open
the same at any time after the ratification of this ordinance,
first giving ten days' notice thereof, of the time and place,
in one or more of the newspapers published in Washington
and Tarboro'; and the said books, when opened, shall be
kept open for the space of thirty days, at least, and as long
thereafter as the commissioners first above named shall
direct, and the said first commissioners shall have power to
call on and require all persons empowered to receive subscriptions of stock, at any time, and from time to time, as
a majority of them may think proper, to make return of
subscriptions of stock by them respectively received. *(margin: Duties of commissioners.)*

5. *Be it further ordained*, That whenever the sum of
ten thousand dollars shall be subscribed in the manner and
form aforesaid, the subscribers, their executors, administrators or assigns, shall be, and they are hereby declared
incorporated into a company by the name and style of the
Washington and Tarboro' Railroad Company, and by that
name shall be capable, in law and equity, of purchasing,
holding, selling, leasing and conveying estates, real, personal
and mixed, and acquiring the same by gift or devise, so far as
shall be necessary for the purposes embraced within the
scope, object and intent of their charter, and no further;
and shall have perpetual succession, and by their corporate
name may sue and be sued, plead and be impleaded in any *(margin: To be declared incorporated when $10,000 is subscribed.)*

court of law and equity in this State, and may have and
use a common seal, which they may alter and renew at
pleasure, and shall have and enjoy all other rights and
immunities which other railroad corporate bodies may, and
of right do exercise, and make all by-laws, rules and regulations that are necessary for the government of the corporation, or effecting the object for which it was created, not
inconsistent with the Constitution and laws of this State.

Stockholder . 6. *Be it further ordained,* That it shall be the duty of
the commissioners named in this ordinance for receiving
subscriptions in Washington, or a majority of them, as
soon as the sum of ten thousand dollars shall have been
subscribed, in manner aforesaid, to give public notice thereof, and at the same time to call a general meeting of the
stockholders, giving at least fifteen days' notice of the time
and place of meeting: a majority of the stockholders
being represented in person, or by proxy, shall proceed to
Directors. elect a President and Treasurer, and six Directors, out of
the number of stockholders; and the said Directors, shall
have power to perform all the duties necessary in the government of the corporation, and the transaction of its
business: and the persons elected as aforesaid, shall serve
such period, not exceeding one year, as the stockholders
may direct: and, at that meeting, the stockholders shall
fix on the day and place or places where the subsequent
Officers. election of President, Treasurer and Directors shall be
held, and such election shall, thenceforth, be annually
made; but if the day of the annual election of officers
should, under any circumstances, pass without an election,
the corporation shall not thereby be dissolved, but the
officers formerly elected shall continue in office until a new
election takes place.

Mode of their election. 7. *Be it further ordained,* That the election of officers
aforesaid, shall be, by ballot, each stockholder having as
many votes as he has shares in the stock of the company,
and the person having the greatest number of votes polled,
shall be considered duly elected to the office for which he
is nominated, and at all elections and upon all votes taken

at any meeting of the stockholders, upon any by-law or any of the affairs of the company, each share of the stock shall be entitled to one vote, to be represented either in person or by proxy; and proxies may be verified in such manner as the by-laws of the company may prescribe.

8. *Be it further ordained,* That the Board of Directors may fill any vacancies that may occur in it during the period for which they have been elected, and in the absence of the President, may appoint a President, *pro tempore,* to fill his place.

9. *Be it further ordained.* That the Board of Directors may call for the sums subscribed as stock in said company in such instalments as the interest of said company may, in their opinion, require. The call for each payment shall be published in one or more newspapers of the State, for one month before the day of payment, and on failure of any stockholder to pay each instalment as thus required, the Directors may sell, at public auction, on a previous notice of ten days, for cash, all the stock subscribed for in said company by such stockholder, and convey the same to the purchaser at the said sale, and if the said sale of stock does not produce a sum sufficient to pay off the incidental expenses of the sale, and the entire amount owing by such stockholder to the company for such subscription of stock, then, and in that case, the whole of such balance shall be held as due at once to the company, and may be recovered of such stockholder, or his executors, administrators or assigns, at the suit of said company, either by summary motion in any court of superior jurisdiction in the county where the delinquent resides, on previous notice of ten days to said subscriber, or by action of assumpsit, in any court of competent jurisdiction, or by warrant before a Justice of the Peace, when the sum does not exceed one hundred dollars; and in all cases of assignment of stock before the whole amount has been paid to the company, then, for all sums [due] on such stocks, both the original subscriber and all subsequent assignees, shall be liable to the company, and the same may recovered as above described.

Debts of stockholders.

10. *Be it further ordained.* That the debt of the stockholders due to the company for stock therein, either as original proprietor, or first or subsequent assignee, shall be considered as of equal dignity with judgments in the distribution of assets of a deceased stockholder by his legal representatives.

Certificates of stock.

11. *Be it further ordained.* That said company shall issue certificates of stock to its members, and said stock may be transferred in such manner and form as may be directed by the by-laws of the company.

Capital stock authorized to be increased $100,000.

12. *Be it further ordained,* That the said company may, at any time, increase its capital stock to a sum sufficient to complete said road, not exceeding the additional sum of one hundred thousand dollars, by opening books of subscription of new stock, or borrowing money on the credit of the company, and the mortgage of its charter and works, and the manner in which the same shall be done, in either case, shall be prescribed by the stockholders.

Contracts by the President and Secretary.

13. *Be it further ordained,* That all contracts or agreements, authenticated by the President and Secretary of the Board, shall be binding on the company, with or without a seal; such a mode of authentication shall be used as the company, by their by-laws, may adopt.

Right of company to purchase real estate

14. *Be it further ordained.* That the said company may purchase, in fee, or for a term of years, any lands, tenements or hereditaments, which may be necessary for said road, or for the erection of depositories, storehouses, houses for the officers, servants or agents of the company, or for workshops or foundries, to be used by the company, or for procuring stone or other material necessary to the construction of the road or effecting transportation, and for no other purposes whatever.

Rights of company in constructing the road.

15. *Be it further ordained,* That the company shall have the right, when necessary, to construct the said railroad across any public road or along the side of any public road: *Provided,* That the said company shall not obstruct any public road without constructing one equally as good and as convenient as the one taken by the company.

16. *Be it further ordained,* That when any lands or right of way may be required by the company for the purpose of constructing their road, building warehouses, waterstations, workshops or depositories, and for want of agreement as to the value thereof, or from any other cause, the same cannot be purchased from the owner or owners, the same may be taken at a valuation to be made by a jury of good and lawful men, to be summoned by the Sheriff of the county in which the land required by the company may lie; and in making the said valuation, the said jury shall take into consideration the loss or damage which may occur to the owner or owners in consequence of the land or right of way being surrendered, and the benefit or advantage he, she or they may receive from the erection of said road, and shall state particularly the value and amount of each; and the excess of loss or damage over and above the advantage and benefit shall form the measure of valuation of the land or right of way: *Provided, nevertheless,* That if any person or persons over whose lands said roads may pass, or the company should be dissatisfied with the valuation thus made, then, and in that case, either party may have an appeal to the next court of the county, to be held thereafter; and the Sheriff shall return to said court the verdict of [the] jury, with all the proceedings thereon, and the lands or right of way so valued by the jury shall vest in the company so long as the same may be used for the purposes of said railroad, so soon as the valuation be paid, or if refused, paid over to the Clerk of the County Court: *Provided, further,* That the right of condemnation shall not authorize the said company to invade the dwelling house, yard, garden or graveyard of any individual without his consent. *(Right to condemn property in cases of disagreement.)*

17. *Be it further ordained,* That the right of said company to condemn land in the manner described in the above section, shall extend to the condemnation only of one hundred feet on each side of the main track of the road, and from the centre of the same, except in case of deep cuts and fillings, when the said company shall have *(Amount to be condemned.)*

14

power to condemn as much in addition thereto as may be
necessary for the purpose of constructing said road, and
the company, in like manner, shall have power to condemn
and appropriate land for the building of depots and shops,
not exceeding five acres in any one lot or station.

Rights of trans-
portation

18. *Be it further ordained,* That the said company shall
have the exclusive right of conveyance or transportation
of persons, goods, merchandise and produce over said road,
at such charges as may be fixed by a majority of the
directors.

Profits.

19. *Be it further ordained,* That the profits of the company, or so much thereof as the Board of Directors may
deem advisable, shall, when the affairs of the company will
permit, be annually or semi-annually divided among the
stockholders in proportion to the stock each may own.

Notice of pro-
cess.

20. *Be it further ordained,* That notice of process upon
the President, or any of the directors thereof, shall be
deemed and taken to be due and lawful notice of service
upon the company.

Powers con-
struct branch
roads.

21. *Be it further ordained,* That the company shall
have power to construct branches of said road to connect
with any other road that may be constructed east of the
Wilmington and Weldon Railroad, and any contract that
may be entered into with any other railroad company by
the President and Directors of said company, after the
consent of a majority of the stockholders first obtained,
shall be binding on the company.

Authority to
issue $50,000 in
bonds bearing
7 per cent.
interest.

22. *Be it further ordained,* That it may be lawful for
the Washington and Tarboro' Railroad Company to make
and issue bonds to an amount not exceeding fifty thousand
dollars, to be signed by the President of said company,
under the common seal of the same, in sums of five hundred dollars each, bearing interst at the rate of seven per
cent. or less per annum, to be paid semi-annually.

Security for the
bonds.

23. *Be it further ordained,* That to secure the faithful
payment of said bonds, it may and shall be lawful for the
President and Directors of the Washington and Tarboro'
Railroad Company to make, execute and deliver to such

person as the company may select or appoint, a deed of trust or mortgage, under the common seal of said company, wherein shall be conveyed to the person thus appointed trustee, the road, property, income and franchise of said company, acquired or to be acquired, conditioned for the payment of the interest and final redemption of said bonds.

24. *Be it further ordained*, That all officers of the company, and servants, and persons in the actual employment of the company, may be, and they are hereby exempt from performing ordinary military duty, (except in case of insurrection or invasion,) working on public roads and serving as jurors. *Employees exempt from militia duty.*

25. *Be it further ordained*, That all the work hereby required, shall be executed with due diligence, and if it be not commenced within four years after the ratification of this ordinance, then this charter shall be void. *Charter to expire unless the work is commenced within four years.*

26. *Be it further ordained*, That this ordinance shall be in force from and after its ratification, and shall be regarded as a public ordinance. [*Ratified the 7th day of February, 1862.*]

AN ORDINANCE TO AUTHORIZE THE TREASU- [No. 10.] RER TO ISSUE TREASURY NOTES.

Be it ordained by the Delegates of the people of North Carolina, in Convention assembled, and it is hereby ordained by the authority of the same, That the Public Treasurer be, and he is hereby authorized to issue any amount of Treasury notes, now on hand, not exceeding one hundred and twenty thousand dollars, above the denomination of twenty dollars: *Provided,* Said notes shall bear no interest: *And provided, further,* That this amount shall be a part of the three millions heretofore ordered to be issued. [*Ratified the 4th day of February, 1862.*] *Treasury notes on hand above the denomination of $20, to be issued.*

[No. 11.] A RESOLUTION IN RELATION TO THE MINTS.

Authorities to
place the Mints
in operation.

Resolved, That in the opinion of this Convention, it is of the highest importance to the interests of the Confederate States, that the Mints situated within their limits should be placed in operation at the earliest practicable period, and that the Senators and Representatives in Congress be requested to use their best exertions to obtain this object. [*Ratified the 7th day of February, 1862.*]

[No. 12.] RESOLUTION RESPECTING THE PAY OF THE THIRTY-EIGHTH REGIMENT OF NORTH CAROLINA VOLUNTEERS.

Pay rolls to be
made out from
date of accep-
tance of com-
panies.

Resolved, That the pay rolls of the companies of the thirty-eighth regiment of North Carolina Volunteers be made out and received from the date of the acceptances of the companies respectively. [*Ratified the 8th day of February, 1862.*]

[No. 13.] AN ORDINANCE CONCERNING THE LEVYING OF TAXES BY THE COUNTY COURTS.

Taxes for
county and
school purposes.

1. *Be it ordained by the Delegates of the people of North Carolina, in Convention assembled, and it is hereby ordained by the authority of the same,* That the Chairman of the County Court, and where there is no Chairman, the County Court Clerk of each and every county in this State, shall, by public notice, convene the Justices of the County Courts at their respective court houses on the first Monday in May, 1862; and a majority of the Justices being present, they shall proceed to levy taxes for county purposes, and may, in their discretion, as now provided by law, levy the taxes for school purposes; and the Clerk of the respective County Courts, shall, in such cases, enter the proceedings of said Justices on the minute docket of said County

Courts, as a part of the record of said courts thus convened
in special session: *Provided*, That in counties holding
regular terms of their County Courts in said month of May,
or the first Monday of June, the levy hereby required
shall be made at such regular term.

2. *Be it further ordained*, That the act of the last extra Repeals act of
session of the General Assembly, entitled "An Act to General Assembly.
enlarge the powers of the County Courts for raising revenue for county purposes;" which requires the Justices of
the several County Courts, at their first court after the
first day of January in every year, to levy a tax for county
and school purposes, &c., be, and the same is hereby modified and repealed, so far as the same may apply to the
present year, 1862.

3. *Be it further ordained*, That this ordinance shall Termination of
expire and be inapplicable after the year 1862. this ordinance.

4. *Be it further ordained*, That those counties in which Taxes levied in
their County Courts have already levied taxes for county ignorance of this ordinance.
and school purposes, and in those counties in which they
may hereafter levy the same in ignorance of the provisions
of this ordinance, the same shall be void and of no effect.
[*Ratified the* 10*th day of February,* 1862.]

A RESOLUTION TO PRINT AN ORDINANCE.   [No. 11.]

Resolved by the Delegates of the people of North Caro- 300 copies to be
lina, in Convention assembled, and it is hereby ordained printed.
by the authority of the same, That the Secretary of State
be authorized and directed to have printed three hundred
copies of the ordinance this day passed, entitled "an ordinance concerning the levying of taxes by the County
Courts," and forward one copy each to the Sheriff, County
Court Clerk and Chairman of the County Court of each
and every county in the State. [*Ratified the* 10*th day of
February,* 1862.]

[No. 15.] AN ORDINANCE TO AUTHORIZE THE HOLDING OF A COURT OF OYER AND TERMINER, AT WAYNESVILLE, IN HAYWOOD COUNTY.

Court to try persons for high crimes.

1. *Be it ordained by the Delegates of the people of North Carolina in Convention assembled, and it is hereby ordained by the authority of the same,* That His Excellency, the Governor of the State be, and he is hereby authorized and requested to issue a commission to any one of the Superior Court Judges of this State, to hold a court of *Oyer* and *Terminer*, at Waynesville, in the county of Haywood, for the purpose of trying the persons now in jail at that place, charged with high crimes, which Judge, when so commissioned, shall be clothed with all the powers necessary for the trial and punishment of such offenders, their accomplices, aiders and abettors.

Duties of the Judge appointed.

2. *Be it further ordained,* That the said Judge shall appoint a day, as early as practicable, for holding the said court, and shall give notice of the time appointed to the Solicitor of the District and the Sheriff of the county, and shall direct the Sheriff to notify three or more Justices of the Peace to meet at the office of the County Court Clerk of said county, and issue a *venire* to attend the said court: and the Sheriff shall summons them to attend at the time appointed, at the Court House of the said county, and the Judge shall cause the grand jury to be drawn from the said *venire*, who shall serve as grand jurors, to pass upon any bill or bills which may be sent before them, and the remainder of the *venire* shall, unless excused by the court, serve as traverse jurors. The said court shall have power to order, if necessary, a further *venire* in said cases.

Rules and regulations.

3. *Be it further ordained,* That the same rules and regulations shall govern the said court that are used at the regular terms, as to the duties of the Judge, the Solicitor, the Sheriff, and all others concerned in the said causes of trial, and all under the same pay, &c.

4. *Be it further ordained,* That this ordinance shall be in force from and after its ratification. [*Ratified the* 10th *day of February,* 1862.]

AN ORDINANCE GRANTING BOUNTY TO CER- [No. 16.] TAIN NORTH CAROLINA VOLUNTEERS.

1. *Be it ordained by the Delegates of the people of North*   To receive boun-
Carolina in Convention assembled, and it is hereby ordained   ties authorized
by the authority of the same, That the volunteers from this   and 10th of
State in the military service of the Confederacy, where   May.
North Carolina is or may be credited for the same by the
Confederate Government, are justly entitled to, and should,
therefore, receive the bounty authorized by the acts of the
eighth day of May, A. D., 1861, and of the tenth day of
May, 1861, whether the same volunteered first to the State
or directly to the Confederate Government: *Provided,
however,* That the officers of all volunteers directly to the
Confederate States shall make such returns as the Governor may require.

2. *Be it further ordained,* That the Governor be author-   Paymaster to
ized and requested to direct the paymaster to pay all vol-   pay the boun-
unteers who may not have received the same, such bounty   ties.
as they are declared to be entitled to by the above section of
this ordinance.   [*Ratified the 10th day of February, 1862.*]

AN ORDINANCE SUPPLEMENTAL TO AN ORDI- [No. 17]
NANCE, RATIFIED AT THE PRESENT SESSION
OF THIS CONVENTION, ENTITLED "AN ORDI-
NANCE IN ADDITION TO AND AMENDMENT
OF AN ACT OF THE GENERAL ASSEMBLY,
RATIFED THE 15th DAY OF FEBRUARY, 1861,
ENTITLED AN ACT TO INCORPORATE THE
CHATHAM RAILROAD COMPANY, AND TO
REPEAL AN ACT SUPPLEMENTAL THERETO,
RATIFIED THE 23rd OF FEBRUARY, 1861,"
AND AUTHORIZING CERTAIN PERSONS TO
OPEN BOOKS OF SUBSCRIPTION TO THE
CAPITAL STOCK OF SAID COMPANY.

1. *Be it ordained by the Delegates of the people of North*   Books of sub-
Carolina, in Convention assembled, and it is hereby ordained   scription to be
by the authority of the same, That an act of the General   opened.

Assembly, entitled "An act to incorporate the Chatham Railroad Company," be amended by adding to section 2nd, the following: "And a majority of said general commissioners shall be competent to transact business; and in the mean time it shall be lawful for books of subscription to said stock to be opened in the city of Raleigh, under the direction of Geo. W. Mordecai, William Henry Jones and Wm. W. Vass, or either of them; in the town of Newbern, under the direction of Ed. Stanly, A. T. Jerkins, W. H. Oliver, or any one of them; in the town of Goldsboro', under the direction of E. A. Thompson, Richard Washington, P. A. Wiley, or any one of them; at Pittsboro', under the direction of H. A. London, John H. Haughton, Jno. A. Womack, or any one of them; at Haywood, under the direction of B. I. Howze, R. K. Smith and I. N. Clegg, or any one of them; at Warrenton, under the direction of J. B. Batchelor, John White, Richard T. Arrington, or any one of them; at Hillsboro', under the direction of William A. Graham, Thomas Webb, P. B. Ruffin, or any one of them; at Smithfield, under the direction of J. W. B. Watson, Edwin Sanders, J. B. Beckwith, or any one of them; at Oxford, under the direction of S. S. Royster, C. H. K. Taylor, R. B. Gilliam, or any one of them; at Louisburg, under the direction of J. J. Davis, J. King, D. S. Hill, or any one of them; at Norfolk, under the direction of S. M. Wilson, Kader Biggs, Jas. Gordon, or any one of them; and at Petersburg, under the direction of W. T. Joynes, R. K. Martin and Geo. D. Baskerville, or any one of them; and said general commissioners shall have power to appoint a Chairman of their body, Treasurer, and all other officers their organization may require, and to sue for and recover all sums of money that ought, under said act, to be recovered by them in the name of said corporation. [*Ratified the 10th day of February, 1862.*]

RESOLUTIONS RELATING TO RE-ENLISTMENT [No. 18.] OF VOLUNTEERS.

Resolved, That in the opinion of this Convention, it is To induce 12 months volunteers to re-enlist. of the utmost importance, in the existing war, that our country shall not lose the services of the gallant volunteers of this State at the expiration of their present term of twelve months, and that such incentives to re-enlist should be held out to them as may induce their return to the army, after a brief interval for visiting their homes.

Resolved, That the Congress of the Confederate States Inducements suggested. should offer such inducements in bounties of money and public land, devolving to them from the United States, within the States of the Confederacy and in the territories, and in pensions, in case of death, disability, and long terms of service, to volunteers enlisting for the war, as will procure the return of those inured to the service, and shall prevail with others to follow their example in filling up the ranks of the army.

Resolved, That any volunteers of this State re-enlisting Privileges of volunteers re-enlisting in the service as herein proposed, should have the privilege of choosing their company officers by companies, and their regimental field officers by the commissioned officers of companies, and in forming regiments, the companies heretofore associated should be kept together where they are filled up in convenient time, and any new companies should be added to the regiment having nearest its complement, when such new company shall be received into the service.

Resolved, That a copy of these resolutions be transmitted by the Secretary of this Convention to the Senators and Representatives of this State in the Confederate Congress, with a request that they bring the subject embraced in them to the consideration of Congress. [*Ratified, the 14th day of February, 1862.*]

15

[No. 19.] RESOLUTIONS CONCERNING THE MANUFAC-TURE OF SULPHUR AND SALTPETRE.

Gov. m c
authorized to
e tabli h a
manufactory.

Resolved, That the Governor be requested, and he is hereby authorized to employ the necessary force and procure the necessary apparatus to manufacture Sulphur and Saltpetre for the use of the State, at such place or places, in or out of this State, as he may deem proper, and that he draw upon the Treasury for the money to meet the expense thereof.

Call upon
Confederate
States for
ammunition.

Resolved, That the Governor be requested to call upon the Government of the Confederate States for a supply of ammunition for our militia and other forces. [*Ratified the 14th day of February,* 1862.]

[No. 20.] RESOLUTION TO RAISE CERTAIN ARTILLERY COMPANIES FOR THE DEFENCE OF WILMING-TON.

Three compa-
nies authorized.

1. *Resolved,* That the Governor be, and he is hereby authorized to raise by volunteer enlistment, not exceeding three artillery companies to serve at the batteries already erected, or which may hereafter be erected on the Cape Fear River, below or at, and in the vicinity of the town of Wilmington, and that the men constituting such companies be entitled to the same bounty, pay and allowances as are by law allowed to the companies in the service of the Confederate States.

Organization
and term of
service.

2. *Be it further resolved,* That the Governor be authorized to appoint Captains and Lieutenants to recruit such companies; the term of service of said companies to be for twelve months, or for three years or the war, unless sooner discharged by the Governor. [*Ratified the 15th day of February,* 1862.]

AN ORDINANCE TO PROVIDE FOR THE ASSUMPTION AND PAYMENT OF THE CONFEDERATE TAX.

1. *Be it ordained by the Delegates of the people of North Carolina, in Convention assembled, and it is hereby ordained by the authority of the same.* That the State of North Carolina will, and doth hereby assume the payment of the tax known as the war tax, levied by the government of the Confederate States upon the people of North Carolina, by an act of the Confederate Congress, ratified on the —— day of ——, 1861.

The State assumes the war tax.

2. *Be it further ordained,* That in order to provide the means for the payment of said tax, the Treasurer of the State is hereby directed to issue Treasury notes, redeemable in five years, to an amount not exceeding a sum sufficient to provide the payment of said tax, which notes shall be made convertible, at the option of the holder, into coupon bonds bearing seven per cent. interest, payable semi-annually, at the Treasury, and such bonds being redeemable ten years after date.

Treasury notes bearing 7 per cent. interest to be issued.

3. *Be it further ordained,* That the Public Treasurer is hereby directed. when called upon to do so, to issue the coupon bonds described in the preceding section of this ordinance for the purpose therein specified.

Issue of coupon bonds.

4. *Be it further ordained.* That the Treasurer is hereby directed to apply the Treasury notes to be issued in obedience to this ordinance, in such manner as may be necessary to the payment of said Confederate tax. which he is hereby directed to make.

Treasurer directed to pay the tax.

5. *Be it further ordained.* That in payment of the Treasury notes hereby authorized, or of the bonds in which they are funded, the funds in the Treasury derived from the ordinary subjects of taxation, shall not be used, but the same shall be raised by a tax on the same subjects of taxation, with the same exemptions that are made in the act of the Confederate Congress imposing said tax, so that the white polls and persons whose estates do not exceed

Subjects to be taxed for paying the Treasury notes above authorized.

five hundred thousand dollars, shall not be liable to pay
any part thereof: and those who have money in possession or in deposit, shall be liable as under said act of Congress.

*addilional tax
Ist to be made
out.*

6. *Be it further ordained.* That for the purpose of
raising the money to pay said Treasury notes or bonds in
which they may be funded, an additional tax list shall be
made out, setting forth only the subjects of taxation
enumerated in the said act of the Confederate Congress,
and the Treasurer shall open and keep a separate account of
said fund. [*Ratified the 17th day of February,* 1862.]

[No. 22.] A RESOLUTION IN FAVOR OF SOLDIERS DE-
TAINED AT RAILROAD STATIONS IN THIS
STATE.

*To furnish vol-
unteers with
food and
lodging.*

Resolved, That the Quartermaster and Commissary at
Raleigh and other railroad connections in this State be
directed, if in their power, to furnish all volunteers who
may be necessarily detained at these places, with food and
lodging so long as they are necessarily detained, and they
shall be allowed the same in the settlement of their accounts.
[*Ratified the 17th day of February.* 1862.]

[No. 23.] AN ORDINANCE TO RAISE NORTH CAROLINA'S
QUOTA OF CONFEDERATE TROOPS.

*The Governor
to call for
volunteers.*

1. *Be it ordained by the Delegates of the people of North
Carolina, in Convention assembled, and it is hereby ordained
by the authority of the same,* That it shall be the duty of
the Governor, from time to time, to issue his proclamation
calling for volunteers to meet the requisitions of the Confederate Government, now made, or hereafter to be made :
Provided, however, That volunteers heretofore in service, re-enlisting, shall have credit for the time they have
served : *Provided, further,* That said volunteers shall not

be [retained in service] for a longer time than three years, and to be sooner discharged in case the present war terminates before the expiration of that time : *And, provided, further,* That the Governor shall not be required to keep in the Confederate service more than the regular quota of North Carolina.

2. *Be it further ordained.* That the Governor shall call upon the counties to furnish, by volunteering, the necessary number of troops, under the present requisition, according to white population (after crediting them with the troops already in the service, for three years or the war, and the volunteers for twelve months) to complete their respective quotas, on or before the 15th of March. 1862.

The counties to supply their quotas.

3. *Be it further ordained.* That the Governor shall require each Captain now in the service. on or before the 15th day of March, 1862. to return to the Adjutant General a list of the officers and men under his command, with the county of the residence of each at the time of his entry into service.

Lists of men now in service to be obtained

4. *Be it further ordained.* That the Governor shall call upon the several captains of volunteer companies from North Carolina in the field for twelve months, or officers in command of companies. to muster their companies for re-enlistment, and shall make known to them the earnest desire of this Convention and the people of North Carolina. that they shall enlist for three years or the war, and in order to forward this purpose, the captains of companies, or officers in command of the company, on the occasion of such muster, shall put the question distinctly to every officer and soldier belonging thereto, whether he will re-enlist for three years or the war, or not : and those agreeing so to re-enlist, he will cause to subscribe a roll containing such obligation, with their names and places of residence at the times of their first entry into service. and the signatures of the persons so re-enlisting shall be as binding as if they had been mustered into service; which lists he will immediately return to the office of the Adjutant General of the State.

Re-enlistment of 12 months volunteers

Volunteers now in
service, per
all-time 5. *Be it further ordained.* That volunteer companies
now in service. re-enlisting, may retain their present
organization. or re-organize at their option; and that all
volunteers not re-enlisting with [their] present organization,
shall be thrown into companies and proceed to elect company
commissioned officers, who shall be commissioned by the
Governor: and the company commissioned officers shall
elect their field officers: *Provided, however,* That the commissions of all officers, company or field, who shall be
re-elected, shall bear the dates of their former commissions.

Recruiting. 6. *Be it further ordained.* That the Governor shall have
power to appoint captains and lieutenants to recruit men
for the service aforesaid, and to organize the men so recruited
into companies and regiments: and the company commissioned officers shall. in all cases. elect their field officers
under the rules now prescribed: *Provided, however,* That
no person shall receive a commission or pay under said
appointments, except as follows: When any person shall
tender forty privates, who, in writing, have agreed to serve
under him, a Captain's commission and pay: and in like
manner for twenty-five privates, a first Lieutenant's commission and pay ; and for fifteen privates, a second Lieutenant's commission and pay.

$50 bounty to
be paid to all
volunteers for
the war 7. *Be it further ordained,* That a bounty of fifty dollars.
deducting the bounty already paid, shall be paid by the
State to all privates, musicians, and non-commissioned officers whose term of service altogether shall be for three
years or the war, to be paid at the following times, to-wit :
To all volunteers now in service at the time of their re-entry
into service: to all now in the service for three years or the
war, at the expiration of their first year's service ; to all new
volunteers, at the time of their entry into service : *Provided.
however,* That any soldier may permit his bounty to remain
in the Treasury and draw the same, with interest, at the
expiration of one year from the time it is due, or at the
time of his discharge: *And, provided further,* That such
payment may be made in Treasury notes, unless otherwise
provided by law. [*Ratified the* 19*th day of February,* 1862.]

AN ORDINANCE TO PROHIBIT, FOR A LIMITED [No. 24.] TIME, THE MANUFACTURE OF SPIRITOUS LIQUORS FROM GRAIN.

1. *Be it ordained by the Delegates of the people of North Carolina, in Convention assembled, and it is hereby ordained by the authority of the same.* That there shall be a tax of thirty cents levied on each gallon of spirituous liquors manufactured in this State, out of any corn, wheat, rye or oats, or any mixture of any or either of them, from the ratification of this ordinance up to the fifteenth day of April next.

Tax of 30 cents per gallon for liquors manufactured previous to 15th April.

2. *Be it further ordained,* That from and after the 15th day of April next, it shall not be lawful for any person in this State to distil any such spirituous liquors, and all persons guilty of violating this section of this ordinance shall, for each and every act of distillation, be guilty of a misdemeanor, and on conviction thereof, shall be fined or imprisoned at the discretion of the court: the fine not to be less than one hundred dollars, or the imprisonment less than thirty days.

Manufacture prohibited after 16th April.

3. *Be it further ordained,* That there shall be levied a tax of one dollar on every gallon of spirituous liquors sold in this State, not of the manufacture of this State: and said tax shall be paid by the seller, and should the seller be a non-resident, then the tax shall be paid by the purchaser.

Tax of $1 per gallon on liquors manufactured out of the State.

4. *Be it further ordained,* That each and every person, when he gives in his list of taxable property, shall also give in, on oath, to the magistrate taking said list, the number of gallons of spirituous liquors on which he is liable to pay taxes under the provisions of this ordinance, under the penalties, liabilities and forfeitures already provided by law in such cases.

Persons to give in number of gallons manufactured in their tax list.

5. *Be it further ordained,* That the tax of one dollar, mentioned in section third of this ordinance, shall not apply to liquors brought into this State before the first day of March next.

6. *Be it further ordained*, That this ordinance shall be in force from and after its ratification, and continue in force until the first day of January, 1863, and no longer, unless re-enacted, modified or amended by the General Assembly. [*Ratified the 21st day of February*, 1862.]

[No. 25.] AN ORDINANCE RELATIVE TO THE EXPENSES
INCURRED BY THE BOARD OF CLAIMS.

Be it ordained by the Delegates of the people of North Carolina in Convention assembled, and it is hereby ordained by the authority of the same, That the Board of Claims may draw upon the Public Treasurer for all incidental expenses necessarily incurred by them in the discharge of their official duties : *Provided,* That such expenses shall not exceed, in the whole, the sum of five hundred dollars : *And, provided further,* That said Board shall, in their final account, render to the State a statement of all monies by them expended under this ordinance. [*Ratified the 21st day of February*, 1862.]

[No. 26.] AN ORDINANCE TO MAKE SOME PROVISION
FOR THE FAMILIES OF SOLDIERS DYING IN
SERVICE.

1. *Be it ordained by the Delegates of the people of North Carolina in Convention assembled, and it is hereby ordained by the authority of the same,* That in case of the death in service of any soldier, intestate, who, at the time of his death was, or shall be, entitled to bounty or any arrearages of pay from this State, such bounty and pay shall belong and be payable to the widow of such intestate soldier, and if there be no widow, to his children, and if there be no children, then to his next of kin as designated in the Statute of Distributions, and in the proportions therein pre-

scribed, and the identity of the person or persons claiming the same, and the degree of relationship of him, her or them, to the intestate as aforesaid, shall be established to the satisfaction of the proper executive or military authorities, according to such regulations and rules as may be prescribed by the said authorities.

2. *Be it further ordained,* That any person who shall False affidavit. wilfully swear falsely in any affidavit, deposition or testimany made or given for the purpose of establishing or endeavoring to establish a claim to any such bounty or pay, shall be guilty of perjury, and upon conviction thereof shall be punished accordingly. [*Ratified the 22d day of February,* 1862.]

AN ORDINANCE CONCERNING THE PAYMAS- [No. 27.]
TER'S DEPARTMENT.

1. *Be it ordained by the Delegates of the people of North* Office of Assistant Paymaster *Carolina, in Convention assembled, and it is hereby ordained* established. *by the authority of the same,* That the twenty-third section of the act of the last session of the General Assembly, entitled "Militia Bill," be amended as follows: "That there shall be one additional officer appointed by the Governor, to be attached as Assistant to the Paymaster's Department, with the rank and pay of a First Lieutenant, who shall be subject to the same chief of the said department, and to the rules and regulations of the same.

2. *Be it further ordained,* That the said office, created by this ordinance, may be vacated by the Governor or the Legislature, whenever the public interest may require. [*Ratified the 24th day of February,* 1862.]

RESOLUTION IN BEHALF OF WM. R. LOVELL. [No. 28.]

Resolved, That the Treasurer of the State pay to Wil- Pays $82. liam R. Lovell the sum of eighty-two dollars, expended by him for the use of the sick soldiers of the eleventh regiment of North Carolina Volunteers, near Manassas, when employed as a nurse in August and September last. [*Ratified the 25th day of February*, 1862.]

[No. 29.] A RESOLUTION IN FAVOR OF THE DOORKEEPERS.

Pays each $25 extra

Resolved, That the Treasurer pay to the Doorkeepers of the Convention twenty-five dollars each, for servants' hire and extra expenses incurred by them during the present session. [*Ratified the 24th day of February*, 1862.]

[No. 30.] AN ORDINANCE TO ENCOURAGE THE MANUFACTURE OF COTTON AND WOOL CARDS.

Offers to loan to parties establishing manufactories the amount of the cost of the same

Be it ordained by the Delegates of the people of North Carolina, in Convention assembled, and it is hereby ordained by the authority of the same, That if any person or persons shall erect buildings and construct machinery, for the purpose of manufacturing cotton and wool cards, and shall make proof to the Governor of the cost of such works, the Governor be, and he is hereby authorized to draw on the Treasurer for sums not exceeding the cost of said works, to be loaned to the owners thereof, on the execution by them of bonds payable to the State, with sufficient security, conditioned to repay such sums at such time as the General Assembly may prescribe, and with such interest as may be required, not exceeding six per cent. per annum: *Provided*, That such advances shall not exceed, in the aggregate, the sum of ten thousand dollars: *And, provided further*, That the cards thus manufactured shall, in the first place, be offered to sale to the citizens of this State. [*Ratified the 25th day of February*, 1862.]

AN ORDINANCE FOR THE PAYMENT OF CLAIMS [No. 31.] AUDITED AND ALLOWED BY THE BOARD OF CLAIMS.

1. *Be it ordained by the Delegates of the people of North* Board of *Carolina in Convention assembled, and it is hereby ordained* Claims— Disbursements. *by the authority of the same,* That the Public Treasurer, upon the warrant of the Governor, pay

To Samuel L. Dill, of Carteret, the sum of thirteen hundred dollars;

To G. W. Dill & Co., of Carteret, fourteen hundred and thirty-three dollars and thirty-three cents;

To W. G. Towler, of New Hanover, thirty-two dollars and fifty cents;

To the Marine Railway Company, of New Hanover, forty-eight dollars and ten cents;

To Dr. Jno. F. Miller, High Point, forty-dollars and ninety cents;

To McIntyre & Brown, New Hanover, sixty-eight dollars and twenty-six cents;

To Thomas II. Allen, of Craven, fifty-seven dollars;

To J. M.'M. Houston & Co., Lincoln, one hundred and four dollars and fifty-seven cents;

To John M. Wolfe, Orange, three dollars and fifty cents:

To E. H. Cunningham, Buncombe, one hundred and forty-three dollars and twenty-five cents;

To Willie Walston, Edgecombe, forty-six dollars and sixty-five cents;

To P. B. Hardin & Co., Alamance, eight dollars and thirty-five cents;

To Dr. W. D. Somers, White Sulphur Springs, Va., five dollars and seventy-five cents;

To E. J. Hale & Sons, Cumberland, five dollars and thirty cents:

To J. H. Wood, Rowan, two hundred and fifty-eight dollars and forty-eight cents;

To John A. Graves, Caswell, twelve dollars and sixty-cents:

To H. C. Stroud, assignee for Frank Harris, Orange, thirty dollars :

To Harris & Howell, New Hanover, sixty dollars ;

To Philip Sale, Greenville County, Va., twenty-five dollars ;

To Joseph Barnham, Northampton, seven dollars ;

To Phifer & York, Cabarrus, one thousand and thirty-nine dollars and sixty-seven cents ;

To Samuel Calvert, Northampton, one hundred and fifty dollars ;

To W. P. Lloyd, Edgecombe, ninety-six dollars and seventy-five cents ;

To Edwin M. Holt, Alamance, two hundred and eighty dollars and thirty-two cents ;

To Jas. Tiddy, Lincoln, forty dollars ;

To William Tiddy, Lincoln, four dollars ;

To John L. Bridgers, Edgecombe, thirty-five dollars and fifty-five cents ;

To D. C. McGregor, Buncombe, six dollars and twenty-five cents ;

To W. H. Stone, Buncombe, fifty-nine dollars and twenty-five cents ;

To R. S. Alexander, Buncombe, thirty-three dollars and three cents ;

To S. H. Christian, Montgomery, thirty-four dollars and seventy-five cents ;

To Isaac Ramsey, Carteret, ninety-six dollars and eighty-four cents ;

To Isaac Ramsey, assignee for L. H. Styron, Carteret, fifteen dollars and sixty cents ;

To Jos. S. Norman, Washington, thirty-three dollars ;

To Dr. Peter E. Hines, Craven, one hundred and two dollars and sixty cents ;

To Dr. A. C. Folson, Brunswick, ninety dollars ;

To J. R. and W. B. Cainer, Martin, forty-six dollars and thirty-eight cents ;

To Dunn & Spencer, Petersburg, one hundred and thirty-three dollars and seventy-six (cents) dollars ;

To Fulton & Price, New Hanover, twenty-two dollars and fifty cents;

To Hart & Bailey, New Hanover, two hundred and sixty-eight dollars and fifty-eight cents;

To John P. Mabry, Davidson, twenty dollars and twenty cents;

To J. B. Whitehurst, Carteret, twenty-four dollars:

To Thomas Duncan & Son, Carteret, eighty-three dollars and seventeen cents;

To E. G. Clark, Wilson, fifty dollars and twenty-five cents;

To Mrs. Sarah A. Reid, Wake, thirty-five dollars;

To Patton & Alexander, Buncombe, two hundred .and forty-three dollars and forty cents;

To A. Mitchell & Son, Craven, two hundred and fifty dollars and twenty-five cents;

To W. W. Smith, Buncombe, two hundred and thirty-five dollars and sixty-one cents;

To Benjamin M. Walker, Washington, one hundred and twenty-eight dollars and ninety cents;

To J. F. Crawley, Beaufort, one hundred and thirty-eight dollars and fifty-five cents;

To Capt. C. M. Avery, Burke, forty-two dollars and fifty cents;

To Dozier & Co., Edgecombe, eighty-one dollars and thirty-five cents;

To Jacob Bachman, Chowan, twenty-four dollars and thirty-five cents;

To J. L. Pennington, Craven, seventy-seven dollars and forty-three cents;

To E. G. Mangum & Co., Orange, one hundred and eight dollars and thirty-nine cents;

To W. C. King, Carteret, two hundred and fifty-eight dollars and eighty cents;

To Geo. W. Ward, Martin, twenty-five dollars:

To W. W. Happer, Halifax, fifty dollars and thirty cents;

To J. J. Jenkins, Cleaveland, twenty-six dollars and thirty-three cents;

To Miller & Foster, Davidson, three hundred and forty-two dollars and twenty-eight cents;

To James A. Washington, Wayne. five hundred and ninety-one dollars and fifty-nine cents;

To Rich'd C. Coher, Northampton, forty-five dollars;

To J. R. Davidson, Iredell. forty-six dollars and ninety-three cents;

To Polk county, five hundred and one dollars and twenty-eight cents;

To Richmond county, three thousand three hundred and nineteen dollars and thirty-one cents;

To Alamance county, two thousand six hundred and ninety-one dollars and fifty-four cents;

To Iredell county, two thousand one hundred and forty-nine dollars and eighty-six cents;

To Macon county, six hundred and fifty-four dollars and seventy-five cents;

To Currituck county, eighty-nine dollars and ninety-one cents;

To Cumberland county, five thousand four hundred and thirty-seven dollars and sixty-six cents;

To Alexander county, five hundred and twelve dollars and eleven cents;

To Lenoir county, six thousand four hundred and ninety-nine dollars and nine cents;

To Jos. H. Neff, New Hanover, one hundred and sixty-three dollars and sixty cents;

To Jerry Drew, and others, Northampton, one hundred dollars;

To Stanly county, two thousand seven hundred thirty-three dollars and thirty-five cents;

To Surry county, two thousand eight hundred and fifty-three dollars and thirty-one cents;

To Caswell county, three thousand nine hundred and forty-three dollars and fifty-seven cents;

To Charles M. Rogers, one hundred and eighty-five dollars and sixty-five cents; and

To Charles H. K. Taylor, assignee, three hundred and twenty-two dollars and sixty-nine cents; *Board of Claims—Disbursements.*

And that said payments be made without prejudice to claims which have been presented and not allowed, on account of commutation pay received from the Confederate States. [*Ratified the 25th day of February,* 1862.]

AN ORDINANCE TO TAX MONEY. [No. 32.]

1. *Be it ordained by the Delegates of the people of North Carolina, in Convention assembled, and it is hereby ordained by the authority of the same,* That hereafter all monies on hand, and all monies on deposit with individuals, or in the banks or other corporations, shall be taxed one-fifth of one per cent., as now imposed on money at interest; and all persons having money in possession or on deposit, as aforesaid, on the first day of April in each and every year, shall be required to list the same when they list other taxable property, under the same liabilities and responsibilities as are now imposed by law for failure or neglect to list other taxable property: *Provided,* That bank notes and Confederate State Treasury notes shall be considered money. *Monies on hand or on deposit taxed one-fifth of one per cent.*

2. *Be it further ordained,* That the provisions of this ordinance shall not apply to those who may have less than one hundred dollars to list. *Less than $100 exempted.*

3. *Be it further ordained,* That this ordinance may be modified or repealed by the General Assembly. [*Ratified the 26th day of February,* 1862.]

AN ORDINANCE REGULATING THE APPOINT- [No. 33.] MENT OF COMPANY OFFICERS.

Be it ordained by the Delegates of the people of North Carolina, in Convention assembled, and it is hereby ordained by the authority of the same, That whenever a vacancy occurs in the commissioned officers of any of the companies *Vacancies to be filled by promotion*

in this State, raised under an act entitled "an act to raise
ten thousand State Troops," or to be raised under the ordinance entitled "an ordinance to raise North Carolina's
quota of Troops," the vacancy shall be filled by promotion
of the officers next in grade in said company ; and whenever
a vacancy shall occur in the office of junior second lieutenant,
the vacancy shall be filled by election by the non-commissioned officers and privates of the company in which such
vacancy occurs. [*Ratified the 26th day of February*, 1862.]

[No. 34.] AN ORDINANCE CONFERRING ON THE COM-
MISSIONERS OF [THE] TOWN OF WILMING-
TON AND OTHER TOWNS CERTAIN POWERS
FOR THE DEFENCE THEREOF.

Authorized to
construct
defensive works

1. *Be it ordained, &c.*, That the commissioners of the
town of Wilmington shall have power to place obstructions
in the river, and to erect or to complete, if already in
process of erection, any work or works upon, or at the
mouth of Cape Fear River, or around, near or within the
said town, which they may deem necessary for the defence
thereof, and also for the like purpose, to purchase cannon,
powder, ball and other munitions of war: *Provided*, That
the said obstructions are placed in the river, with the consent of the Confederate officer in command.

Provision to
meet the
expenses.

2. *Be it further ordained*, That to meet the expenses
which may be incurred under the foregoing section, the said
commissioners shall have power to borrow money upon such
terms and under such regulations as they may adopt, and
to impose such taxes upon the subjects now liable to taxation within said town as may be necessary.

The State
assumes the
expenses
provided the
Confederate
States declines
to assume them

3. *Be it further ordained*, That whenever the commanding officer shall certify that the expenses incurred by the
commissioners under this ordinance were necessary for the
State defence, the same shall be a charge upon the Public
Treasury : *Provided*, That application shall have first been
made to the Confederate Government, and they shall have

failed to assume the payment of the same six months after said application.

4. *Be it further ordained.* That the provisions of this ordinance be extended to the commissioners of the towns of Newbern and Washington, or any other towns that may make the same application, under similar circumstances. [*Ratified the 26th day of February, 1862.*]

Newbern and Washington

AN ORDINANCE TO PROVIDE FOR FUNDING [No. 35.] THE TREASURY NOTES OF THIS STATE, AND FOR OTHER PURPOSES.

1. *Be it ordained, &c.,* That any of the Treasury notes issued or hereafter to be issued under the ordinance of this Convention, ratified the 1st of December, 1861, directing the issue of three millions of Treasury notes, as well as those issued by an ordinance of the present session, entitled "An ordinance to provide for the assumption and payment of the Confederate Tax," may be funded at the will of the holder in coupon bonds of the State, to be prepared by the Treasurer, and payable 20 years after date, or sooner, at the pleasure of the State, and bearing interest at the rate of eight per cent. per annum, payable semi-annually at the Treasury, or in six per cent. bonds of the State, payable 30 years after the 1st of January, 1862, interest payable semi-annually, exchangeable in Treasury notes, at the option of the holder, from time to time, until the Treasury notes fall due, said bonds being of the denominations of $500 and $1,000, in equal proportions.

May be funded in Coupon Bonds.

2. *Be it further ordained.* That all taxes due to the State or to counties, and for school purposes, or taxes for the poor, and all payments for entries of public lands, and all other dues to the State, and all fines and forfeitures for the use of the State or counties, shall be paid in Treasury notes of the State or of the Confederate States, or in the notes of such of the solvent banks of this State as shall receive and continue to receive and pay out as money at par the

May be paid for taxes

17

Treasury notes of this State, or in gold or silver coin: and it shall be the duty of the Treasurer to issue instructions to the Sheriffs and tax collectors in the several counties on this subject, and it shall not be lawful for any Sheriff or collector to receive taxes in any other funds than as directed by the Treasurer under this ordinance.

May be re-issued

3. *Be it further ordained,* That all the Treasury notes funded in bonds, or paid into the Treasury for taxes or other public dues, may be re-issued in payment of the debts of the State, or in exchange for six per cent. bonds of the State, on application of the holder at any time before the notes fall due: *Provided,* That the Treasury notes issued to pay the Confederate tax shall not be used to pay the

Account to be kept of those re-issued or funded

debts of the State: and the Treasurer and Comptroller shall each keep an account of all notes re-issued and those refunded in bonds, from to time, and the date of such transaction, and particularly noting the interest on each bond when taken up, and the amount of interest due on each bond when exchanged for Treasury notes, and in all cases shall charge the party receiving such bonds with the interest due at the time of delivery.

Authorizes the issue of $1,500,000 in Treasury notes

4. *Be it further ordained,* That as the exigencies of the public service may, in the opinion of the Governor, require before the first day of January, 1863, the Public Treasurer is authorized and required to issue other Treasury notes as aforesaid, not exceeding in amount the further sum of fifteen hundred thousand dollars, and that the said notes shall be prepared, signed and issued as in the said ordinance, ratified on the first day of December, 1861.

Outstanding amount limited

5. *Be it further ordained,* That the aggregate amount of said Treasury notes outstanding at any one time, and of the bonds given in exchange for or discharge of Treasury notes as aforesaid, shall not exceed the amount of such notes authorized by law heretofore, or in this ordinance.

$5, $10 and $20 to be issued in exchange for $50 and $100 notes

6. *Be it further ordained,* That it shall be the duty of the Treasurer, as soon as convenient, to issue Treasury notes of the denominations of five, ten and twenty dollars in equal amounts, instead of, and to exchange for, any of

the Treasury notes heretofore issued, not bearing interest, of the denominations of fifty and one hundred dollars, on the application of the holders of said notes, and when so taken up or exchanged, the said notes of fifty and one hundred dollars shall be cancelled, and the same shall be noted by the Treasurer on his books and on the books of the Comptroller.

7. *Be it further ordained,* That if any one shall falsely forge, or knowingly pass, or offer to pass, any false, forged, or counterfeited paper, purporting to be a Treasury note or bond of this State, he shall be liable to indictment in the Superior Courts in the county in which such offence may be committed, and on conviction thereof, shall suffer all the pains and penalties, according to the 59th section of the 34th chapter of the Revised Code. *Punishment for counterfeiting or passing counterfeits.*

8. *Be it further ordained,* That in addition to the Treasury notes heretofore issued, it shall be the duty of the Treasurer to issue one million of dollars, in small denominations, to-wit: four hundred thousand dollars in the denomination of two dollars, four hundred thousand dollars in the denomination of one dollar, one hundred thousand dollars in the denomination of fifty cents, fifty thousand dollars in the denomination of twenty-five cents, twenty-five thousand dollars in the denomination of twenty cents, and twenty-five thousand dollars in the denomination of ten cents, payable on the first day of January, 1866, to be used in liquidation of any claims against the State to persons willing to receive the same, but not to be funded in bonds of the State, but shall be receivable in payment of taxes or other public dues; and he shall keep an accurate account of the issues, from time to time, made under this section of this ordinance. *$1,000,000 to be issued in small denominations.*

9. *Be it further ordained,* That no bank receiving the Treasury notes of this State, as contemplated in the section of this ordinance, shall be required to receive, or have on hand at any one time, more than two-fifths of the capital stock of such bank in said notes. *Banks receiving Treasury notes.*

132   STATE CONVENTION.   [Feb., 1862.

Revised acts of the General Assembly and Convention ratified.

10. *Be it further ordained,* That so much of the act of the General Assembly, entitled "An Act to provide ways and means for the defence of the State," ratified September 18th, 1861, as authorizes the issue of one million dollars of the denominations of two dollars, one dollar, fifty cents, twenty-five cents, twenty cents, ten cents and five cents, and also the ordinance of the Convention, ratified December 1, 1861, directing the issue of three millions of dollars of Treasury notes, and the ordinance to provide for the assumption and payment of the Confederate tax, as well as all the issues of Treasury notes and bonds under said act and ordinances, are hereby ratified and confirmed.

The Treasurer and Comptroller to employ persons to sign the notes.

11. *Be it further ordained,* That in the event of the inability of the Public Treasurer or Comptroller to sign the Treasury notes authorized by law to be issued as speedily as the demands on the Treasury may require, then it shall be lawful for either of them to employ some discreet person, by and with the advice and consent of the Governor, to sign and countersign the said notes, whose names shall be published in the newspapers in the city of Raleigh.

12. *Be it further ordained,* That this ordinance may be repealed or modified by the General Assembly, but so as not to affect any transactions had or rights vested under the same, previous to such modification or repeal. [*Ratified the 26th day of February,* 1862.]

ORDINANCES, AND RESOLUTIONS

PASSED BY

THE STATE CONVENTION

OF

NORTH CAROLINA.

Fourth Session in April and May, 1862.

ORDINANCES AND RESOLUTIONS

OF THE

STATE CONVENTION

OF

NORTH CAROLINA.

FOURTH SESSION IN APRIL AND MAY, 1862.

AN ORDINANCE IN REGARD TO HOLDING THE [No. 1.]
COURTS IN AND FOR THE COURTY OF HERT-
FORD.

Be it ordained by the Delegates of the people of North May be held in
Carolina, in Convention assembled, and it is hereby ordained Winton.
by the authority of the same, That hereafter, until otherwise provided by the General Assembly, the Courts of
Pleas and Quarter Sessions, and also the Superior Courts
of Law and Equity, for the county of Hertford, may be
held in the town of Winton, or in any convenient building
within one-half mile of the corporate limits of said town.
[*Ratified the 26th day of April, 1862.*]

RESOLUTION IN REGARD TO A CERTAIN CLAIM [No. 2.]
IN FAVOR OF J. R. DAVIDSON.

WHEREAS, At the second extra session of this Conven- Preamble
tion an ordinance was passed for the payment of claims
audited and allowed by the Board of Claims, in which was

18

included a claim of J. R. Davidson, of Iredell county, for forty-six dollars and ninety-three cents: and, *whereas*, it appears that this same claim has been paid to the claimant by the Paymaster General's Department; therefore,

Treasurer to withhold payment

Be it resolved, That the Treasurer of the State withhold the payment of ·the said claim of forty-six dollars and ninety-three cents to said Davidson. [*Ratified the 26th day of April*, 1862.]

[No. 3.]   RESOLUTIONS CONCERNING THE COUNTY OF
BURKE.

7th section of the Revenue Act not to apply to Burke.

1. *Resolved*, That the seventh section of an act passed at the second extra session of the General Assembly of 1860–'61, entitled "An Act concerning Revenue," shall not apply to the county of Burke, but that the Court of Pleas and Quarter Sessions of said county, next ensuing, shall be allowed to carry into effect the provisions of said section.

Privilege of the Clerk of the County Court.

2. *Be it further resolved*, That the Clerk of the County Court of said county, shall be allowed until the 25th day of August, 1862, to deliver to the Sheriff of said county a fair and accurate copy of the tax lists, as required by the 20th section of said Revenue Act.

Justices.

3. *Be it further resolved*, That twelve Justices of the Peace in and for said county of Burke, shall form a quorum and have full power to assess and levy taxes, and transact all other county business, provided a majority of said Justices cannot be assembled.

4. *Be it further resolved*, That the first and second of these resolutions shall expire and be inapplicable after the year 1862. [*Ratified the 1st day of May*, 1862.]

AN ORDINANCE FOR THE RELIEF OF THE BANKS [No. 4.] OF THIS STATE.

Be it ordained by the Delegates of the people of North Carolina in Convention assembled, and it is hereby ordained by the authority of the same, That during the continuance of the present war, the stockholders of all the Banks in this State, located at places occupied or in danger of being occupied by the enemy, whereby the holding of the stock-holders' annual meetings thereat may be impracticable, or quite uncertain; may, if they deem it expedient, hold general meetings at other times and places than those specified in their several charters, which meetings shall be called in the manner prescribed in their charters and by-laws, respectively, and held at places as convenient as may be practicable to their respective locations: and the President and Directors of any such Banks who are now in office may continue therein until a meeting of its stock-holders shall be held and their successors shall be elected. [*Ratified the 2d day of May,* 1862.]

Authorizes stockholders in Banks to change their places of meeting under certain circumstances.

AN ORDINANCE TO PROVIDE FOR COLLECTING [No. 5.] THE TAX ON SPIRITUOUS LIQUORS MANU-FACTURED OR SOLD IN THIS STATE, IM-POSED BY AN ORDINANCE OF THIS CON-VENTION, WHICH WAS RATIFED ON THE 21st DAY OF FEBRUARY, 1862.

1. *Be it ordained by the Delegates of the people of North Carolina, in Convention assembled, and it is hereby ordained by the authority of the same,* That the Sheriffs of the several counties in this State be, and they are hereby authorized and directed to collect from the distillers of spirituous liquors in their respective counties, the tax of thirty cents per gallon "on each gallon of spirituous liquors manufactured in this State." and of "one dollar on every gallon of spirituous liquors sold in this State not

To be collected at the same time as other taxes.

Oaths to be administered to distillers and sellers.

the manufacture of this State," imposed by an ordinance of this Convention, ratified February 21st, 1862, at the time they, the said Sheriffs, collect the other taxes as required by law. The said Sheriffs shall have power and authority to administer oaths to such distillers or sellers as to the quantity distilled or sold by them, in all cases where the same shall not have been regularly listed at the time for listing taxables, and shall collect the tax on the same, in all cases, whether the said distillers or sellers may have listed the same at the time they listed their other taxables or not. The Sheriffs of the several counties shall, on paying into the Treasury the taxes of their respective counties, render a separate account or schedule of the tax collected from this source, to be set forth by the Comptroller in his annual official report.

Punishment for refusing to list on oath the quantity of liquor made or sold.

2. *Be it further ordained,* That any person who shall refuse or neglect to state, on oath, to the Sheriff as before provided, the quantity of spirituous liquors manufactured or sold, as the case may be, and to pay the tax on the same, as imposed by law, shall be guilty of a misdemeanor, and in addition to the liability to pay double taxes, such person shall be indicted in the County or Superior Courts, and on conviction, shall be fined at the discretion of the court; and it is hereby made the duty of the grand juries to present all such delinquents, and it is also made the duty of the Sheriffs of the several counties of this State to report to the County or State Solicitor for their counties, the names of all persons that may fail or refuse to render a statement, under oath, to the Sheriff, of the quantity of spirituous liquors manufactured or sold by them; and this ordinance shall be given in charge to the grand juries of the courts of the several counties of this State; and any Sheriff of any county in this State who shall fail or refuse to discharge the duty imposed on him by this ordinance, shall be indictable as for a misdemeanor, and, on conviction, fined at the discretion of the court. [*Ratified the 2nd day of May,* 1862.]

AN ORDINANCE CONCERNING THE ELECTION [No. 6.] OF GOVERNOR.

WHEREAS, By the construction which, in practice, has been given to the Constitution of the State, the Speaker of the Senate, in case of a vacancy in the office of Governor, shall exercise the powers of Governor by virtue of his office as Speaker, and without vacating the same, which said office of Speaker must cease and determine with that of the incumbent as a Senator, upon the election of his successor in the next succeeding Senate, and the same construction would apply to the succession of the Speaker of the House of Commons to the exercise of the powers of Governor; and *whereas*, according to this construction, a vacancy will take place in the office of Governor from and after the day of the next election on the first Thursday in August next, until the first day of January, A. D., 1863, against which it is the duty of this Convention to provide; therefore, *Preamble.*

1. *Be it ordained by the Delegates of the people of North Carolina in Convention assembled, and it is hereby ordained by the authority of the same,* That the person who shall be elected Governor of this State at the next regular election on the first Thursday in August next, as now provided for by law, shall also fill the office and discharge the duties of Governor of this State from the second Monday of September until his successor shall be qualified. *Governor elect in August to take his seat on the 2d Monday in September.*

2. *Be it further ordained,* That the proper returning officers of every county, shall, as soon as the result of the election is known in his county, transmit to the Secretary of State a statement of the votes taken in his county for Governor, which statement shall be made up from the poll books of his county, as is now prescribed by law. *Duties of returning officers.*

3. *Be it further ordained,* That the Secretary of State, the Treasurer and Comptroller, shall, on the fourth Thursday in August next, in the presence of the Governor, proceed to examine said returns, and ascertain and declare what person shall have received the greatest number of *Vote to be counted on the 4th Thursday in August.*

votes, whereupon the Governor shall issue his proclamation, declaring such person duly elected Governor of this State from the second Monday of September, A. D., 1862, until his successor shall be qualified.

Governor elect to take the oath of office on the 2 Monday in September.

4. *Be it further ordained,* That the person so declared and proclaimed Governor as aforesaid, shall, on the second Monday of September, A. D., 1862, appear before some Judge of the Supreme Court, or some one of the Judges of the Superior Courts of Law, and take and subscribe the oath now prescribed by law for qualification of Governor of this State, and shall immediately enter upon the discharge of the duties of his office, which oath, so taken and subscribed, shall be filed in the office of Secretary of State.

Gov. Clark to continue in office till his successor is qualified.

5. *Be it further ordained,* That His Excellency, Henry T. Clark, shall continue to hold the office and discharge the duties of Governor of this State from the first Thursday in August until the second Monday in September next, or until his successor shall be qualified, as fully and to all intents and purposes, as he has heretofore done, and shall receive the usual salary, in proportion to his extended term of service. [*Ratified the 2nd day of May,* 1862.]

[No. 7.] RESOLUTION TO PROVIDE FOR THE PROMPT COLLECTION OF THE TAX IMPOSED ON THE MANUFACTURE AND SALE OF ARDENT SPIRITS.

Comptroller to have printed 300 copies of Ordinance, and to forward to county officers.

Resolved, That the Comptroller be authorized and directed to have immediately printed three hundred copies of the ordinance passed this day, entitled "An Ordinance to provide for the collecting of the tax on spirituous liquors manufactured or sold in this State, imposed by an ordinance of the Convention, ratified on the twenty-first day of February, 1862," and forward a copy to the Sheriff, County Court Clerk, the Chairman of the County Court and the County Solicitor, for each and every county in the State. [*Ratified the 2nd day of May,* 1862.]

AN ORDINANCE TO PAY THE REV. MORRIS H. [No. 8.] VAUGHAN FOR CERTAIN SERVICES.

Be it ordained by the Delegates of the people of North Pays $100.
*Carolina, in Convention assembled, and it is hereby ordained
by the authority of the same,* That the Public Treasurer
pay the Rev. Morris H. Vaughan one hundred dollars for
services as Chaplain at Roanoke Station from the 25th of
June to the 25th of August, 1861, and that the same be
allowed the Treasurer in the settlement of his accounts.
[*Ratified the 5th day of May,* 1862.]

AN ORDINANCE AMENDATORY OF AN ORDI- [No. 9.] NANCE TO RAISE NORTH CAROLINA'S QUOTA OF CONFEDERATE TROOPS, PASSED AND RATIFIED THE 19TH OF FEBRUARY, A. D., 1862.

1. *Be it ordained by the Delegates of the people of North* The bounty to
Carolina, in Convention assembled, and it is hereby ordained N. C. Troops.
by the authority of the same, That under the 7th section of
"An Ordinance to raise North Carolina's quota of Con-'
federate Troops," the bounty to privates, musicians and
non-commissioned officers shall be paid as follows: To all
volunteers between eighteen and thirty-five years of age,
for three years or the war, including those accepted directly
by the Confederate Government, where North Carolina is
or may be credited for the same; to all volunteers between
eighteen and thirty-five years of age for a less term, re-enlisting or continuing in service for three years or the war,
including their former term, by virtue of the Conscription
Act of Congress; and to all persons, substitutes excepted,
mustered into companies already organized, or organized
into companies preparatory to active service by virtue of
said Act of Congress: *Provided, however,* That the officers
of all volunteers directly to the Confederate Government,
claiming the said bounty, shall make such returns as the
Governor may require.

2. *Be it further ordained,* That the bounty to those now in service shall be due presently and be paid according to seniority of regiment.

3. *Be it further ordained,* That the Governor be, and he is hereby directed to discharge all volunteers over thirty-five years of age not yet transferred to the Confederate Government, that may desire a discharge.

4. *Be it further ordained,* That all volunteers for three years or the war that have volunteered or may volunteer before the seventeenth of this month, and shall continue in service for the war, shall be entitled to the bounty of fifty dollars as heretofore paid, although they may be over thirty-five years of age. [*Ratified the 6th day of May,* 1862.]

[No. 10.] AN ORDINANCE EXEMPTING THE PROPERTY OF DELINQUENT SOLDIERS FROM DOUBLE TAXES.

WHEREAS, At the time prescribed by law for listing taxable property in this State, many of its citizens were in the military service of their State and of the Confederate States, and in consequence thereof failed to give in their lists of taxable property; therefore,

Be it ordained by the Delegates of the people of North Carolina, in Convention assembled, and it is hereby ordained by the authority of the same, That the Sheriffs of the respective counties in this State are hereby instructed to collect no more taxes from such delinquents than they would have been liable for had they rendered in their lists of taxables according to law. [*Ratified the 7th day of May,* 1862.]

AN ORDINANCE TO AUTHORIZE THE PUBLIC [No. 11.]
TREASURER TO PAY REV. F. V. HOSKINS
FOR SERVICES AS CHAPLAIN OF THE SEV-
ENTH REGIMENT OF NORTH CAROLINA VOL-
UNTEERS.

Be it ordained by the Delegates of the people of North Pays $100.
Carolina, in Convention assembled, and it is hereby ordained
by the authority of the same, That the Treasurer pay the
Rev. F. V. Hoskins the sum of one hundred dollars for his
services as Chaplain to the Seventh Regiment of North
Carolina Volunteers, from the twenty-ninth of August,
1861, to the twenty-ninth of October, 1861, while prisoners
of war, and that he be allowed the same in the settlement
of his public account. [*Ratified the 7th day of May,* 1862.]

AN ORDINANCE IN REGARD TO THE BOARD [No. 12.]
OF CLAIMS.

Be it ordained by the Delegates of the people of North To report to
Carolina, in Convention assembled, and it is hereby ordained bly.
by the authority of the same, That after the adjournment
of this Convention, the Board of Claims, during their
continuance in office, may report the result of their action
on such claims as they allow to the General Assembly;
and the General Assembly is hereby authorized to pass,
finally, upon such claims, and make provision for their
immediate payment. [*Ratified the 7th day of May,* 1862.]

RESOLUTION IN FAVOR OF ALAMANCE COUNTY. [No. 13.]

Resolved, That the Public Treasurer pay to the County Pays $536 31.
of Alamance the sum of five hundred and thirty-six dollars and thirty-one cents, allowed by the Board of Claims,
as reported by the said Board this day, by way of making
up the proper sum, which ought to have been allowed in
the report in February last. [*Ratified the 7th day of*
May, 1862.]

19

[No. 14.] AN ORDINANCE TO AMEND AN ORDINANCE, EN-
TITLED "AN ORDINANCE TO SECURE TO CER-
TAIN OFFICERS AND SOLDIERS THE RIGHT
TO VOTE."

Returning
officers allowed
20 days to
receive the vote
of soldiers.

1. *Be it ordained by the Delegates of the people of North
Carolina, in Convention assembled, and it is hereby ordained
by the authority of the same,* That the proper returning
officers of every county in this State shall include in their
returns the votes of officers and soldiers given in any
election in which they may be entitled to vote by law, if
received within twenty days after they are cast, and the
said returning officers shall not make up their returns and
declare the result of said elections until the expiration of
twenty days as aforesaid.

To transmit the
vote to the Gov-
ernor within 8
days.

2. *Be it further ordained,* That the proper returning
officer of every county shall, within eight days after the
period fixed for comparing the returns, transmit to the seat
of government and deliver to the proper officer a statement
of votes given in his county for Governor, which statement
shall be made in the manner and form now required by
law.

3. *Be it further ordained,* That the Governor be directed to make known, by proclamation, the provisions of
the ordinance securing to officers and soldiers the right to
vote. [*Ratified the 8th day of May,* 1862.]

[No. 15.] AN ORDINANCE TO AUTHORIZE THE PAYMENT
OF CERTAIN CLAIMS ALLOWED AND RE-
PORTED BY THE BOARD OF CLAIMS.

Board of
Claims—
Disbursements.

*Be it ordained by the Delegates of the people of North
Carolina in Convention assembled, and it is hereby ordained
by the authority of the same,* That the Treasurer be, and he
is hereby authorized to pay the following claims out of any
monies in the Treasury not otherwise appropriated, and
shall be allowed the same in the settlement of his account:

To Bladen county, six thousand eight hundred and sixty dollars and twenty-three cents ;

To Mecklenburg county, six thousand one hundred and seventy-seven dollars and three cents;

To Davidson county, four thousand one hundred and eighty-nine dollars and thirty cents ;

To B. F. Biddle, one hundred dollars;

To Ellis & Mitchell, sixty dollars and forty-two cents ;

To Samuel R. Bunting, seven dollars and twelve cents ;

To J. F. Post, L. H. Bowen, W. T. J. Vann, G. L. Dudley, J. L. Wooster, Thad. H. Nichols, Thos. E. Lawrence, D. E. Bunting, Thos. J. Southerland. Sam'l Shepard. W. P. Elliott, Thomas C. Moore, D. K. F. Everitt, H. A. Martindale, S. A. Story, J. A. Wright, James W. Lippitt, John W. Zimmerman, and R. J. Howard thirty-seven dollars and fifty-two and two-third cents each:

To Pitt county, seven thousand three hundred and sixty-one dollars and sixty-seven cents:

To Gates county, five thousand six hundred and twenty-one dollars and fifty-four cents ;

To Rutherford county, four thousand three hundred and seventy-one dollars and eighty-two cents ;

To Ashe county, one thousand one hundred and eighty-one dollars and eighty cents ;

To Hyde county, one thousand nine hundred and seventy-six dollars and fifty-nine cents ;

To Wilson county, three thousand six hundred and eighty-nine dollars ;

To Caldwell county, one thousand two hundred and one dollars and forty-two cents ;

To J. H. Neff, one hundred and sixty dollars and thirty-eight cents ;

To Rockingham county, three thousand eight hundred and fifty-one dollars and ninety-six cents ;

To W. H. & R. S. Tucker, one hundred and fifty-seven dollars and fifty-two cents ;

To James Cassiday, eighty-eight dollars and fifty cents ;

To Capt. J. W. Francis, one thousand one hundred and sixty-two dollars and ninety-five cents ;

To J. R. Love, twenty-four dollars;

To B. D. Morrill, seven dollars;

To J. S. Williams, seventy-eight dollars and sixty-six cents;

To J. P. Flannagan, (Iredell,) twelve dollars;

To Columbus county, six thousand six hundred and thirty-three dollars and fifty-one cents;

To Anson county, seven thousand seven hundred and twenty-one dollars and eighty-two cents;

To Franklin G. Pitt, two hundred and thirty-five dollars and seventy cents;

To Charles Green, fifty-seven dollars;

To Stanly county, six hundred and twenty-five dollars and twenty-nine cents;

To B. M. Walker, one hundred and forty-five dollars;

To J. M. Israel, two hundred and twenty-three dollars and one cent;

To W. H. Cunningham, one hundred and nine dollars and eighty-five cents;

To James Wilson, two hundred and eighty-two dollars and forty-four cents;

To John J. Long, Trustee for Virginia A. Johnson, seventy-five dollars;

To J. W. Bennett & J. W. McDaniel, Administrators of W. T. Bennett, deceased, eighteen dollars and twenty cents;

To Dr. E. S. Carter, forty-three dollars and twenty-four cents;

To Bertie county, six hundred and fifty-four dollars and twenty-two cents;

To Daughtry, Cox & Co., fourteen dollars and twenty-eight cents;

To Freer & Elliott, fourteen dollars and fifty cents;

To W. R. Blanchard, eleven dollars and thirty-eight cents;

To Barrow & Co., thirteen dollars and ninety-three cents;

To J. H. Dalton, twenty dollars;

To Dr. L. R. Sanders, three hundred and ninety dollars;

To John Cohoon, fifty-nine dollars and ninety-two cents; Board of Claims—Disbursements.

To James Cassiday, Assignee, four hundred and twenty-five dollars;

To A. S. Crowson, twenty-seven dollars and twenty-five cents;

To E. Stanly, four dollars and fifty-one cents;

To Jas. B. Gordon, sixteen dollars and fifty-seven cents;

To H. Hoer, two dollars and twenty-five cents;

To John K. Currie, thirty-four dollars;

To Dr. John W. Davis, one hundred and sixty-three dollars and twenty-five cents;

To D. Pender & Co., one hundred and one dollars and forty-seven cents;

To McNair, Bro. & Co., one hundred and thirty-seven dollars and fifty cents;

To B. H. Merriman, three hundred dollars and ninety-nine cents;

To W. F. & T. J. Strayhorn, twenty-nine dollars and eighty-two cents;

To Dr. Joseph Commander, seventy-eight dollars;

To Samuel C. Bryson, seven hundred and forty-five dollars and twenty-three cents;

To Worth & Daniel, thirty-seven dollars and sixty-four cents;

To R. T. Clark, sixty dollars; and

To Montgomery county, two thousand nine hundred and seventy-six dollars and eighty-nine cents. [*Ratified the 8th day of May, 1862.*]

AN ORDINANCE TO AUTHORIZE THE STOCK-HOLDERS OF THE MINERS' AND PLANTERS' BANK, OF MURPHY, TO ESTABLISH AN AGENCY OR BRANCH EAST OF THE BLUE RIDGE. [No. 16.]

1. *Be it ordained by the Delegates of the people of North Carolina, in Convention assembled, and it is hereby ordained by the authority of the same,* That the stockholders of the To be established wherever stockholders may designate.

Miners' and Planters' Bank, at Murphy, shall have the right to establish an Agency or Branch east of the Blue Ridge at such place as said stockholders in general meeting may agree upon.

Subscription to be paid within 12 months.

2. *Be it further ordained,* That hereafter all the subscriptions to the capital stock of said bank shall be paid in full within twelve months from the date of subscription.

3. *Be it further ordained,* That this ordinance shall be in force from and after its passage. [*Ratified the 9th day of May,* 1862.]

[No. 17.] AN ORDINANCE TO PROVIDE FOR THE COLLECTION OF TAXES, AND FOR OTHER PURPOSES.

A majority of the Justices of the Peace remaining in the county to be considered a majority of the whole.

1. *Be it ordained by the Delegates of the people of North Carolina, in Convention assembled, and it is hereby ordained by the authority of the same,* That in all cases requiring a majority of the Justices of the Peace to discharge any duty pertaining to their offices as members of the several Courts of Pleas and Quarter Sessions of this State, a majority of those at the time remaining in the county, shall be deemed and held to be a majority within the purview of the ordinance of this Convention or of the acts of the General Assembly.

2. *Be it further ordained,* That in those counties which have failed to make provision for the collection of revenue according to the seventh section of an act passed at the second extra section of the General Assembly of 1860–'61, entitled "An Act concerning Revenue," it shall be the duty of the Courts of Pleas and Quarter Sessions, at their next session, to proceed to execute said section.

Clerks allowed till 25th Aug. to return tax lists to Sheriffs

3. *Be it further ordained,* That the Clerks of said counties shall be allowed until the twenty-fifth of August, eighteen hundred and sixty-two, to deliver to the Sheriffs of said counties, copies of the tax lists so required by the twentieth section of said Revenue Act.

4. *Be it further ordained,* That this ordinance shall be in force for thirty days only after the rise of the next General Assembly. [*Ratified the 9th day of May,* 1862.]

AN ORDINANCE IN ADDITION TO AND AMEND- [No. 18.] MENT OF AN ORDINANCE, ENTITLED "AN ORDINANCE IN REGARD TO THE SUPPLY OF SALT."

SECTION 1. *Be it ordained by the Delegates of the people of North Carolina in Convention assembled, and it is hereby ordained by the authority of the same,* That said Commissioner may agree with the owners of any land upon which he has or may hereafter erect salt works, for the purchase or lease of said land, and also for the purchase of the right of way to and from said works, and also of any canals which may be necessary for the purpose of obtaining wood to supply the State Salt Works; and in case of disagreement with the owner of such land, or if the owners be *feme coverts, non compos,* under age or out of the State, said Commissioner, upon giving five days notice to the owner of said land, if he be a citizen of the State, may apply to any Justice of the Peace for the county in which the land is situated, who shall thereupon issue his warrant to the Sheriff, or any other lawful officer of said county, to summon twelve freeholders to meet on the land to be valued on a day to be expressed in such warrant, which shall be within ten days from issuing thereof, and the Sheriff or other officer, upon the receipt of any such warrant, shall summon such freeholders accordingly, and when met, provided as many as seven be present, he shall administer an oath to them that they will impartially estimate the value of such land as may be required by said Commissioner for the use of said works, and their proceedings shall be reduced to writing under their hands and seals, and returned by the officer to the next Superior Court of law for the county in which the land is located; but if either the Commissioner or the

Powers conferred upon the Salt Commissioner in regard to purchase of land for salt works, &c.

owner of the land shall be dissatisfied with the assessment of the freeholders, either party may appeal to the same term of the court to which the return is directed to be made, and have his appeal entered at that term; but such appeal shall in no way hinder or delay the operations of the Salt Commissioner, and whenever such value shall be ascertained, it shall be paid by the Commissioner, out of the sum heretofore placed at his disposal, and the title to said lands shall vest in the State during the continuance of the present war.

Authority to bore for salt and establish salt works.

SEC. 2. *Be it further ordained,* That said Commissioner is authorized to bore for salt and establish salt works wherever in the State he may deem it advisable or expedient; and if, upon examination and experiment, he shall be satisfied that salt or salt water is found in sufficient quantities to make salt, he may contract with the owner of the land, for the renting, leasing or purchasing of said land or salt mines, and in case of disagreement, the toll, rent or value of said land or mines shall be ascertained as prescribed in the first section of this ordinance, and upon payment of such assessed rent or value, the title to said land or mines shall vest in the State during the war.

Free negroes to be employed upon the salt works.

SEC. 3. *Be it further ordained,* That said Commissioner is authorized to employ the free negroes of the State upon the salt works, and to give them the rations and pay of soldiers; and in the event he shall not be able to obtain such a number as may be needed for said works, the Governor is hereby required to impress into the service of the State as many able bodied free negro men as may be necessary for that purpose.

Persons making salt exempt from military duty.

SEC. 4. *Be it further ordained,* That all persons who are or may be employed in making salt, under contract with the salt commissioner, shall be exempt from military duty and militia service while so employed.

SEC. 5. *Be it further ordained,* That this ordinance shall take effect from its passage, and shall be subject to alteration, modification or repeal by the General Assembly.

[*Ratified the 9th day of May,* 1862.]

AN ORDINANCE PROVIDING FOR AN INCREASE [No. 19.]
OF THE SALARIES OF THE TREASURER,
COMPTROLLER AND SECRETARY OF STATE
FOR THE YEAR 1862.

SECTION 1. *Be it ordained by the Delegates of the peo- Treasurer to have $2,500, ple of North Carolina in Convention assembled, and it is Comptroller $1,500, and hereby ordained by the authority of the same,* That for the Secretary of State $1,000. year eighteen hundred and sixty-two, the Treasurer of this State shall receive as his salary, twenty-five hundred dollars, the Comptroller shall receive fifteen hundred dollars, and the Secretary of State shall receive one thousand dollars.

SEC. 2. *Be it further ordained,* That this ordinance Ordinance expires Dec. shall expire and cease to be in force and operation on the 31, 1862 thirty-first day of December, one thousand eight hundred and sixty-two. [*Ratified the 9th day of May,* 1862.]

AN ORDINANCE TO ENLARGE THE POLICE [No. 20.]
POWERS OF THE SEVERAL CORPORATE
TOWNS IN THIS STATE.

SECTION 1. *Be it ordained by the Delegates of the peo- Authorize corporate au- ple of North Carolina, in Convention assembled, and it is thorities to regulate, hereby ordained by the authority of the same,* That the restrain or prohibit the sale corporate authorities of the several cities and towns of this of spirituous liquors State, shall have power to regulate, restrain or prohibit within their corporate limits, or within one mile thereof, the sale of spirituous liquors: *Provided, nevertheless,* That where any tax shall have been paid for an annual license, it shall be the duty of the Commissioners to make a *pro rata* compensation for such time as such license shall be suspended.

SEC. 2. *Be it further ordained,* That for the violation Commissioner to prescribe of any by-law, or rule made by said Commissioners in pur- penalties for violation of suance of this ordinance, they may prescribe penalties not laws on the subject exceeding one hundred dollars, for each offence, to be

recovered before the Mayor, Intendant. or Magistrate of
Police. without any stay of process. mesne or final, and
when judgment shall be given for any such penalty, the
party convicted may, unless the penalty and costs be paid,
be immediately committed to jail for the space of thirty
days. or until payment thereof shall be made, or else the
Mayor, Intendant, or Magistrate of Police may issue execution therefor: *Provided,* That any party dissatisfied
with such judgment shall be allowed an appeal to the next
Court of Pleas and Quarter Sessions for the county, upon
entering into recognizance with sufficient security for his
appearance to said court. and also for the penalty and
costs.

SEC. 3. *Be it further ordained,* That this ordinance may
be altered, modified or repealed by the General Assembly.
[*Ratified the 9th day of May,* 1862.]

[No. 21.] AN ORDINANCE TO INCORPORATE THE SAPONA IRON COMPANY.

Powers of
Company

SECTION 1. *Be it ordained by the Delegates of the people
of North Carolina, in Convention assembled, and it is hereby
ordained by the authority of the same,* That John C. Washington, James E. Hoyt, George Washington and William
Murdock, their associates, successors and assigns, be, and
they are hereby created and constituted a body politic and
corporate, by the name and style of "The Sapona Iron
Company," and as such, shall have perpetual succession.
and may have and use a common seal, and change the same
at pleasure : may sue and be sued, plead and be impleaded
in any Court of Law and Equity ; shall have power to
make all such by-laws and regulations (not inconsistent with
the existing laws and Constitution of this State,) as may
be deemed necessary for the government of said company.
which shall be binding thereon, and shall have, exercise
and enjoy all the rights and privileges of a body corporate
necessary or requisite to carry on the business of exploring

and mining coals, iron ores, and other minerals, and smelt-
ing, manufacturing, transporting and vending the same;
and shall also have power to purchase, lease, hold, convey
and dispose of any estate, real and personal: *Provided*,
That said corporation shall, at no one time, hold more than
twenty thousand acres of land.   Said company shall have,
also, the right, power and authority, to build and construct
roads and ways, whether tram, plank or turnpike, and to
charge the same as to them may seem advisable, for the
transportation to, from, or between their mines and furnaces
of iron, coal, coke, ores, minerals and materials, and also to
construct such canal or canals and drains as may be required
or needful for the supply of water to their furnaces, the
transportations of coal, ores, and materials as aforesaid,
and the drainage of their mines: and that any or all of
such roads, canals and drains shall be opened to the use of
the public upon the payment of such reasonable tolls and
compensation, and subject to such rules and regulations as
said corporation may, by their by-laws, establish.

SEC. 2. *Be it further ordained*, That when any lands or
rights of way may be required by said company for constructing said road, canals or drains, and for the want of
agreement as to the value thereof or for any other cause, the
same cannot be purchased of the owner or owners, the same
may be taken and the value thereof ascertained, as follows,
viz: On application by the company to any Justice of the
Peace, for the county where said land or right of way may
be situate, it shall be his duty to issue his warrant to the
Sheriff of said county to summon a jury of at least five
freeholders, to meet on the land, on a day expressed in
such warrant, not less than five nor more than twenty days
thereafter, and the Sheriff, on the receipt of said warrant,
shall summon the jury, and when met, shall administer an
oath or affirmation to them, if three or more appear, that
they will impartially value the land in question, or right of
way.   The proceedings of such jurors accompanied by a
description of the land or right of way, shall be returned
under their hands and seals, or a majority of them, by the

*Authority to
seize and con-
demn lands or
rights of way.*

Sheriff to the Clerk of the County Court, there to remain
as a matter of record, and on the payment of said valuation, the lands or right of way so valued shall vest in said
company so long as the same shall be used for the purpose
of said road, canal or drain: *Provided*, That the location
of said road, canal or drain, shall not interfere with any
grave-yard, or with any house, houselot or garden, without
the consent of the owners thereof: *Provided, further*, That
no more land shall be condemned for the purposes aforesaid,
than twenty feet in width on either side from the centre of
said road, canal or drain: *And, provided further*, That if
any person or persons over whose land said roads, canals
or drains may pass, or said company shall be dissatisfied
with the valuation of said jurors, either party may have an
appeal to the Superior Court of the county in which the land
lies; but such appeal shall not delay or interrupt the use
or enjoyment of said right of way by said company.

SEC. 3. *Be it further ordained*, That the capital stock
of said company may be divided into such number of shares
and of such amount for each share as the stockholders
thereof may, in general meeting, direct: *Provided*, That
the capital stock of said company shall not exceed one
million of dollars: that said shares shall be personal property, and certificates thereof may be issued and the same
may be made transferable and assignable, and liable to
assessment, forfeiture and sale by the Board of Directors
in such manner as the by-laws of said corporation may
prescribe.

SEC. 4. *Be it further ordained*, That the affairs of said
company shall be managed by a Board of Directors, all of
whom shall be stockholders of said company, and citizens
of the Confederate States. Said Board of Directors shall
be composed of such number and shall be elected by the
stockholders in such manner as the by-laws shall direct,
and who shall choose one of their number to be President of
the Board, and of the Company: three of said Board shall
constitute a quorum to transact business, of whom the
President or one appointed by him to fill his place, shall

always be one; they shall have power to fill vacancies which may happen in their body, and until the first election of directors by the stockholders the said John C. Washington, James E. Hoyt, George Washington and William Murdock shall constitute the Board of Directors of said company, with full power and authority to exercise all the corporate powers thereof.

SEC. 5. *Be it further ordained,* That general meetings of the stockholders may be called and held as the by-laws may prescribe ; that to constitute a meeting there must be present, in person or by proxy, (the proxy being a stockholder) a number holding a majority of the stock, each share of which shall entitle the holder to one vote, and every act shall require the sanction of a majority of the votes present.

SEC. 6. *Be it further ordained,* That this ordinance shall take effect and be in force from and after its passage, and shall continue in force for the period of ninety-nine years. [*Ratified the 9th day of May,* 1862.]

General meeting of stockholders.

RESOLUTION PROVIDING FOR THE PRINTING OF THE JOURNALS OF THE CONVENTION.

[No. 22.]

Resolved, That when this Convention shall be dissolved, that the Principal Secretary have printed five hundred copies of its Journal : two copies to be furnished to every former and present member of the Convention : two to each of the Secretaries of the Convention ; two to the Library of the University ; one to each County and Superior Court Clerk's office in the State; and one-half of the residue to be deposited in the office of the Secretary of State; and the other half in the public Library of the State : and that the Secretary be allowed the sum of one hundred dollars for transcribing the Journal. [*Ratified the 9th day of May,* 1862.]

500 copies to be printed.

[No. 23.] AN ORDINANCE IN RELATION TO ELECTORS
OF THE SENATE.

Qualification
of voters for
Senators

*Be it ordained by the Delegates of the people of North
Carolina, in Convention assembled, and it is hereby ordained
by the authority of the same,* That every free white man,
of the age of twenty-one years, being a native or natural-
ized citizen of the Confederate States, who has been an
inhabitant of the State for twelve months, and of the district in which he proposes to vote six months next before
the day of any election, and shall have paid public taxes,
shall be entitled to vote for a member of the Senate for
the district in which he resides.   [*Ratified the* 10th *day of
May,* 1862.]

[No. 24.] AN ORDINANCE FOR THE RELIEF OF SUCH
PERSONS AS MAY SUFFER FROM THE DE-
STRUCTION OF THE RECORDS OF HERTFORD
COUNTY, OCCASIONED BY THE BURNING OF
THE COURT HOUSE AND CLERK'S OFFICES
OF SAID COUNTY.

Preamble

WHEREAS, In the month of March last, the Court House
of Hertford county was burned by the public enemy, and
with the Court House was destroyed the Clerk's offices of
said county, whereby the former records of wills, deeds,
and other instruments of writing were destroyed, and the
title of the citizens of said county to their property, if not
entirely lost, are in a loose and confused condition: and,
whereas, the county of Hertford met with a like misfor-
tune in March, 1830, by having its Court House and records
burnt by some evil disposed person; and, *whereas,* the evil
was then remedied, as far as practicable, by the passing an
act by the General Assembly at its session of 1830–'31,
entitled "an act for the relief of such persons as may
suffer from the destruction of the records of Hertford
county occasioned by the burning of the Court House and

Clerk's offices of said county," chapter LXVIII, and the
further passage of another act of the General Assembly,
at its session of 1831–'32, entitled "an act in addition to
an act passed at the last session of the General Assembly
of this State, in relation to the burning of the records of
the county of Hertford," chapter XCVI; and, *whereas*,
the like calamity has happened to the county of Hertford
again by the burning of the Court House and the public
records of the county by the public enemy: therefore,

*Be it ordained by the Delegates of the people of North
Carolina, in Convention assembled, and it is hereby ordained
by the authority of the same,* That the same and identical
provisions of the before recited acts of the General Assembly of the session of 1830–'31, chapter LXVIII: and of
the session of 1831'–32, chapter XCVI be, and the same
are hereby revived and re-enacted, and made applicable to
the present wants, necessities and condition of the county
of Hertford, to all intents and purposes, and with the same
force and effect as if the two before recited acts of the
General Assembly were herein specially set forth with all
and every of their parts and provisions. [*Ratified the 10th
day of May, 1862.*]

Previous acts of General Assembly to apply in this instance.

RESOLUTION IN FAVOR OF ROBERT TOWLES. [No. 25.]

Resolved, That Robert Towles be allowed twenty dollars
for his attendance on this Convention during the present
session of this Convention, and that the Public Treasurer
be directed to pay the same. [*Ratified the 10th day of
May, 1862.*]

Pays $20

AN ORDINANCE TO LEGALIZE THE LAYING OF TAXES IN UNION COUNTY. [No. 26.]

*Be it ordained by the Delegates of the people of North
Carolina in Convention assembled, and it is hereby ordained
by the authority of the same,* That the act of the Justices

Action of Justices declared legal.

of the Peace of Union county, laying a tax for the year
eighteen hundred and sixty-two, though done by less than
a majority, be, and the same is hereby declared to be legal.
[*Ratified the* 10th *day of May.* 1862.]

[No. 27.] AN ORDINANCE TO ENABLE THE WESTERN RAILROAD COMPANY TO COMPLETE THEIR ROAD.

Part of 5th section of Act of General Assembly repealed.

SECTION 1. *Be it ordained by the Delegates of the people of North Carolina, in Convention assembled, and it is hereby ordained by the authority of the same,* That that part of section fifth of an act of the Legislature of North Carolina, ratified February 16th, eighteen hundred and sixty-one, entitled "an act to enable the Western Railroad Company to extend their road from the Coalfields to the North Carolina Railroad," which requires the President of said road to certify to the Governor that the Company has purchased the iron rails, chairs and spikes, and will, forthwith, proceed to lay down and complete each section of ten miles before said company is entitled to receive the sum of one hundred thousand dollars, be, and the same is hereby repealed.

Extension of the lien.

SEC. 2. *Be it further ordained,* That the lein created by the said act, shall extend to and cover both the eastern and western divisions of said road, and all the other property of said corporation. [*Ratified the* 10th *day of May,* 1862.]

[No. 28.] AN ORDINANCE TO REPEAL THE NINTH SECTION OF THE CHARTER OF THE CHERAW AND COALFIELDS RAILROAD, AS AMENDED BY THE LEGISLATURE OF 1860-'61.

Repeals 9th section of the Cheraw and Coalfields Railroad Charter.

Be it ordained by the Delegates of the people of North Carolina, in Convention assembled, and it is hereby ordained by the authority of the same, That section nine of an act passed in 1861 to revive and continue in force an act to incorporate the Cheraw and Coalfields Railroad Company, passed at the session of 1856-'7, chapter sixty-six, be, and the same is hereby repealed: *Provided*, That the said Cheraw and Coalfields Railroad Company shall do as much work and expend as much money in the construction of their road north of the Wilmington, Charlotte and Rutherford Railroad as they do south at the same time ; and said road shall not cross, tap or connect with the said Wilmington, Charlotte and Rutherford Railroad further west than twelve miles from the town of Rockingham, and shall, in five years after the close of the present war, complete the road to the Coalfields in Chatham county, or its charter shall thereupon cease and determine. [*Ratified the* 10*th day of May,* 1862.]

AN ORDINANCE REQUIRING THE PUBLIC TREASURER TO REDEEM MUTILATED TREASURY NOTES.   [No. 29.]

Be it ordained by the Delegates of the people of North Carolina, in Convention assembled, and it is hereby ordained by the authority of the same, That it shall be the duty of the Public Treasurer, on application by the holders of mutilated Treasury notes, to redeem the same with other notes of like denominations; and that he be required to keep a record of all notes thus redeemed, in a separate book for this purpose, and make a report of the same to the General Assembly. [*Ratified the* 12*th day of May,* 1862.]

To redeem them with notes of same denomination

RESOLUTION FOR THE PUBLICATION OF THE ORDINANCES OF THE PRESENT SESSION OF THE CONVENTION.   [No. 30.]

Resolved, That the Secretary of State cause the Ordinances and Resolutions, passed and ratified at the present

To be published in three ....

21

session of this Convention, to be published in three newspapers printed in the city of Raleigh. [*Ratified the 12th day of May, 1862.*]

[No. 31.] AN ORDINANCE TO AUTHORIZE THE PAYMENT OF CERTAIN CLAIMS ALLOWED BY THE BOARD OF CLAIMS.

Board of Claims— Disbursements.

Be it ordained by the Delegates of the people of North Carolina, in Convention assembled, and it is hereby ordained by the authority of the same, That the Public Treasurer pay to R. D. Williams, of New Hanover, nine hundred and sixty-eight dollars:

To John N. Whitford, of Craven, seven hundred and thirteen dollars and fifty cents:

To Dr. C. Winslow, of Perquimons, one hundred forty-seven dollars and fifty cents:

To Henderson county, two thousand two hundred and seventy dollars and seventy-five cents;

To Kahnweiler & Bro., of Mecklenburg, three hundred and twenty-six dollars:

To Jacob Ludwick, of Cabarras, fourteen dollars and twenty cents;

To Haywood county, six hundred and twenty dollars:

To Iredell county, fifty dollars:

To Alleghany county, one thousand three hundred and seventy-eight dollars:

To D. C. Murray, thirteen dollars and sixty-nine cents; and that he be allowed the same in the settlement of his public accounts. [*Ratified the 12th day of May, 1862.*]

[No. 32.] AN ORDINANCE TO REPEAL AN ORDINANCE PASSED AT THE PRESENT SESSION OF THIS CONVENTION, ENTITLED "AN ORDINANCE AMENDATORY OF AN ORDINANCE TO RAISE NORTH CAROLINA'S QUOTA OF CONFEDER-

ATE TROOPS, PASSED AND RATIFIED THE
NINETEENTH DAY OF FEBRUARY, A. D., 1862,"
AND TO EXTEND THE PROVISIONS AS TO
BOUNTY TO CERTAIN OTHER PERSONS.

SECTION 1. *Be it ordained by the Delegates of the peo-* Annul-
ple of North Carolina, in Convention assembled, and it is ordinance, &c.
hereby ordained by the authority of the same, That an ordinance, entitled "An Ordinance amendatory of an ordinance to raise North Carolina's quota of Confederate
Troops," passed at the present session of this Convention
be, and the same is hereby abrogated and annulled.

SEC. 2. *Be it further ordained,* That a bounty of fifty Designation of
dollars, deducting the bounty already paid and received, persons to whom bounty
shall be paid by the State to all privates, musicians and is to be paid.
non-commissioned officers, as follows: To all volunteers
between eighteen and thirty-five years of age for three
years or the war, including those accepted directly by the
Confederate Government, where North Carolina is or may
be credited for the same : to all volunteers between eighteen and thirty-five years of age for a less term, re-enlisting or continuing in service by virtue of the Conscription
Act of the Confederate Congress for three years or the
war, including their former service : to all persons, substitutes excepted, mustered into companies already organized, or which may be organized into companies preparatory to active service by virtue of the provisions of the
said act of Congress : to all volunteers over thirty-five
years of age who may decline to be discharged under the
provisions of said act of Congress and be retained in the
public service : to all volunteers under eighteen years of
age for three years or the war who shall elect and be
bound to remain in service ; to all persons who have volunteered since the nineteenth day of Februrary, eighteen
hundred and sixty-two.

SEC. 3. *Be it further ordained,* That the commanding Volunteers to
officers of companies, battalions, regiments or legions, the Confederate
volunteering directly to the Confederate Government. States direct.

claiming bounty, shall make out such muster rolls and returns as the Governor may require. [*Ratified the 12th day of May, 1862.*]

[No. 33.] RESOLUTION IN FAVOR OF THE DOORKEEPERS.

· *Resolved,* That the Public Treasurer be directed to pay to John C. Moore and Drewry King, Doorkeepers of the Convention, the sum of fifty-one dollars for discharging the duties of Wm. R. Lovell, Principal Doorkeeper, during his absence of seventeen days, and that the Treasurer be directed to pay the further sum of ten dollars each to Messrs. Moore and King, and also W. R. Lovell, as extra allowance for services as Doorkeepers during the present session. [*Ratified the 12th day of May, 1862.*]

[No. 34.] AN ORDINANCE TO EXEMPT MEMBERS OF THE SOCIETY OF FRIENDS FROM PERFORM-INNG MILITARY DUTY.

To pay $1 ... an equivalent ... t to assist in in the manu-facture of salt r act a nurse

1. *Be it ordained by the Delegates of the people of North Carolina, in Convention assembled, and it is hereby ordained by the authority of the same,* That members of good standing in the Society of Friends, commonly called Quakers, who shall produce a regular certificate of membership, shall be exempt from performing militia duty and military service: *Provided,* That as an equivalent for such exemption from military service, when called for by the proper authorities, they shall pay the sum of one hundred dollars, to be collected by the Sheriffs of the several counties, as other State taxes are collected, to be paid into the State Treasury for the general purposes thereof, and in case they be unable to pay the same, the Governor shall have power to detail them to assist in the manufacture of salt, or to attend in the hospitals of the State. [*Ratified the 12th day of May, 1862.*]

AN ORDINANCE CONCERNING THE COLLEC- [No. 35.] TION OF TAXES IN CERTAIN COUNTIES.

1. *Be it ordained, &c.,* That the Sheriffs of such counties as are or shall be invaded or taken possession of by the enemy, shall severally, at the time prescribed by law, settle their accounts with the Comptroller, so far as they shall have received or collected the State taxes, and the residue of the taxes for which they are chargeable they shall account for and pay into the Treasury at such time as shall be prescribed by the next General Assembly.

Duties of Sheriffs in counties in possession of the enemy.

2. *Be it further ordained,* That it shall not be the duty of the Treasurer, as is now provided by law, to move for summary judgment against such of the aforesaid Sheriffs as shall not have been able to collect and pay over the full amount of taxes with which they are severally chargeable.

The Treasurer not to move for summary judgment.

3. *Be it further ordained,* That the penalties prescribed in the act of the General Assembly, entitled "An Act entitled Revenue," ratified the 23d day of September, A. D., 1861, for the failure to list taxable property, shall not apply to persons living in such counties as have been invaded and taken possession of by the enemy. [*Ratified the 12th day of May,* 1862.

Penalties of Revenue Act not to be enforced.

AN ORDINANCE TO ALLOW CERTAIN PERSONS [No. 36] TO VOTE FOR GOVERNOR IN ANY OTHER THAN THE COUNTIES IN WHICH THEY RESIDE.

SECTION 1. *Be it ordained by the Delegates of the people of North Carolina, in Convention assembled, and it is hereby ordained by the authority of the same,* That any citizen of this State who shall be entitled to vote for Governor in the county wherein he is domiciled, shall be entitled to vote for Governor in any county in this State

Citizens to vote for Governor in any county in the State

SEC. 2. *Be it further ordained,* That it shall or may be lawful for the Sheriffs of the counties in this State, in the

Sheriffs to … are to …

possession of or under the control of the enemy, to compare the polls of their respective counties for Governor and
members of the Legislature at any place in this State they
may think proper.

*more time
for continuing the
war.*

SEC. 3. *Be it further ordained,* That this ordinance shall
be and continue in force for and during the present war,
and no longer, unless sooner repealed or modified by the
General Assembly.   [*Ratified the* 12th *day of May,* 1862.]

[No. 37.] RESOLUTION TO PRINT THE ORDINANCES AND RESOLUTIONS OF THE CONVENTION.

*500 copies to be
printed.*

Resolved, That five hundred copies of the Ordinances
and Resolutions of the Convention be printed and distributed in the same manner as the Journals thereof.   [*Ratified
the* 12th *day of May,* 1862.]

[No. 38.] AN ORDINANCE TO CHARTER THE FLORENCE AND FAYETTEVILLE RAILROAD COMPANY.

*Authorized
capital
$1,500,000.*

SECTION 1. *Be it ordained by the Delegates of the people of North Carolina, in Convention assembled, and it is
hereby ordained by the authority of the same,* That for the
purpose of establishing a communication by railroad, between Fayetteville, N. C., and Florence, S. C., the formation of a corporate company with a capital of one million
five hundred thousand dollars, to be called the Fayetteville
and Florence Railroad Company, [is hereby authorized]
and when formed in compliance with the conditions hereinafter prescribed, to have a corporate existence as a body
politic.

The route

SEC. 2. *Be it further ordained,* That the said company
be, and the same is hereby authorized to construct a railroad from Fayetteville, N. C., to Florence, S. C., upon
such route as may be determined upon by said company
after the same shall have been formed.

SEC. 3. *Be it further ordained*, That for the purpose of To raise the capital stock. raising the capital stock of said company, it shall be lawful to open books in the town of Fayetteville, under the direction of the following commissioners. to-wit : Augustus W. Steele, David A. Ray, A. A. McKethan, William McL. McCoy and J. M. Rose, and at such other places, and under the direction of such other persons as a majority of the above named commissioners may deem proper, for the purpose of receiving subscriptions to an amount not exceeding one million five hundred thousand dollars. in shares of one hundred dollars each.

SEC. 4. *Be it further ordained*, That the commissioners Books to be opened after 20 days notice, and to be kept open 60 days above named, and all others who may be hereafter authorized as aforesaid, to open books for subscription, shall open the same at any time after the ratification of this ordinance, first giving twenty days notice thereof of the time and place, in one or more of the newspapers in the town of Fayetteville, and the said books, when opened, shall be kept open for the space of sixty days, at least, and the said first named commissioners shall have power to call on and require all persons authorized to receive subscriptions of stock, from time to time. as a majority of them may see proper, to make returns of the subscriptions of stock, by them respectively received.

SEC. 5. *Be it further ordained*. That whenever the sum Privilege of the company after $100,000 are subscribed of one hundred thousand dollars shall be subscribed by solvent men. in manner and form aforesaid, the subscribers, their executors, administors, or assigns, shall be, and are hereby declared incorporated into a company by the name and style of the Florence Railroad Company, and by that name shall be capable in law and equity, of purchasing, holding, selling, leasing, and conveying estates, both real and personal, and of acquiring the same by gift or devise, so far as shall be necessary for the purposes embraced within the intent of their charter, and no further, and may, by their corporate name, sue and be sued, plead and be impleaded in any court of law and equity in this State : and may have and use a common seal, which they may

alter and renew at pleasure, and shall have and enjoy all
other rights and immunities which other corporate bodies
may and of right do exercise, and make all such by-laws,
rules and regulations as are necessary for the government
of the corporation, or effecting the object for which it was
created, not inconsistent with the constitution and laws of
this State.

Election of
directors,
&c.

SEC. 6. *Be it further ordained*, That it shall be the
duty of the commissioners named in this ordinance, in Fayetteville, or a majority of them, as soon as the sum of one
hundred thousand dollars shall have been subscribed, in
the manner aforesaid, to give public notice thereof, and at
the same time call a general meeting of the stockholders,
giving at least thirty days notice of the time and place of
meeting, at which meeting a majority of the stockholders
being represented, in person or by proxy, shall proceed to
elect a President and Treasurer, and nine Directors, out of
the number of stockholders, and the said Directors shall
have power to perform all the duties necessary for the government of the corporation and the transaction of the
of the business.   And the persons so elected, as aforesaid,
shall serve such period, not exceeding one year, as the
stockholders may direct, and at that meeting the stockholders
shall fix the day and place or places, where the subsequent
election of President, Treasurer, and Directors, shall be
held, and such elections shall thenceforth be annually
made; but if the day of the annual election of officers
shall, under any circumstances, pass without an election,
the corporation shall not thereby be dissolved, but the officers formerly elected shall continue in office until a new
election takes place.

Mode of election
of officers.

SEC. 7. *Be it further ordained*, That the election of
officers aforesaid shall be by ballot, each stockholder having as many votes as he has shares in the stock of the
company, and the person having the greatest number of
votes polled, shall be considered duly elected to the office
for which he is nominated; and at all elections, and upon
all votes taken, at any meeting of the stockholders upon

any by-law, or any of the officers of the company, each share of stock shall be entitled to one vote, to be represented in person or by proxy, and proxies may be verified in such manner as the by-laws of the company prescribe.

SEC. 8. *Be it further ordained.* That the Board of Directors may fill any vacancies that may occur in it during the period for which they have been elected, and in the absence of the President, may appoint a President, *pro tempore,* to fill his place.

Vacancies.

SEC. 9. *Be it further ordained.* That the Board of Directors may call for the sums subscribed as stock in the said company, in such instalments as the interests of said company may, in their opinion, require. The call for each payment shall be published in one or more newspapers of the State, for one month before the day of payment, and on failure of any stockholder to pay each instalment as thus required, the directors may sell, at public auction, on a previous notice of ten days, for cash, all the stock subscribed for in said company by such stockholders, and convey the same to the purchaser at sale; and if the said sale of stock do not produce a sum sufficient to pay off the incidental expenses of the sale, and the entire amount owing by such stockholder to the company for such subscriptions of stock, then and in that case, the whole of such balance shall be held as due at once to the company, and may be recovered of such stockholder, or his executors, administrators or assigns, at the suit of said company, either by summary motion, in any court of superior jurisdiction in the county where the delinquent resides, on previous notice of ten days to said subscriber, or by an action of assumpsit, in any court of competent jurisdiction, or by warrant before any Justice of the Peace, when the sum does not exceed the sum of one hundred dollars; and in all cases of assignment of stock, before the whole amount has been paid to the company, then for all sums due on such stock, both the original subscribers and the first and all subsequent assignees, shall be liable to the company, and the same be recovered as above described.

The collection of subscriptions

22

Debts due to
stockholders

SEC. 10. *Be it further ordained.* That the debt of the Stockholders due to the Company for stock therein, either as original proprietors, or as first or subsequent assignees, shall be considered as of equal dignity with judgments in the distribution of assets of a deceased stockholder by his legal representatives.

Certificate of
stock

SEC. 11. *Be it further ordained.* That said Company shall issue certificates of stock to its members, and said stock may be transferred in such manner and form as may be directed by the by-laws of the Company.

Authority to
increase the
capital stock.

SEC. 12. *Be it further ordained,* That the said Company may, at any time, increase its capital stock to a sum sufficient to complete said road, by opening books for subscription of new stock, or borrowing money on the credit of the company, and on the mortgage of its charter and works, and the manner in which the same shall be done in either case shall be prescribed by the Stockholders.

SEC. 13. *Be it further ordained,* That said Company shall have power of using any section of said road constructed by them before the whole of the said road is completed, and may charge for transportation thereon.

Contracts and
agreements.

SEC. 14. *Be it further ordained,* That all contracts or agreements, authenticated by the President and Secretary of said road, shall be binding on the Company, either with or without a seal. Such a mode of authentication shall be used as the Company by their by-laws may adopt.

Authority to
purchase real
estate.

SEC. 15. *Be it further ordained.* That the said Company may purchase and have, and hold in fee, or for a term of years, any lands, tenements, or hereditaments, which may be necessary for the said road, or for the erection of depositories, houses for the officers and agents of the Company, or for workshops, or foundries for the Company, or for any other purposes for the furtherance of said road.

Rights of the
company.

SEC. 16. *Be it further ordained,* That the Company shall have the right, when necessary, to construct the said Railroad across any public road, or along the side of any public road: *Provided,* That the said Company shall not obstruct any public road, without first constructing one equally as good and convenient as the one taken by said Company.

SEC. 17. *Be it further ordained,* That when any land or right of way be required by said Company, for the purpose of constructing their road, building warehouses, water stations, workshops or depositories, and for want of agreement as to the value thereof, the same cannot be purchased from the owner or owners, the same may be taken at a valuation, to be made by a jury of good and lawful men, to be summoned by the Sheriff of the county in which the land may lie, and in making the said valuation, the said jury shall take into consideration the loss or damage which may accrue to the owner or owners in consequence of the land or right of way being surrendered, and also any special benefit or advantage, he, she, or they may receive from the erection of the said road, and shall state the value and amount of each, and the excess of loss or damage over and above the advantages, shall form the measure of valuation of said land or right of way: *Provided, nevertheless,* That if any person over whose land the said road may pass, or the Company should be dissatisfied with the valuation thus made, then, and in that case, either party may have an appeal to the Court of the county, to be held thereafter, and the Sheriff return to said Court the verdict of the jury, with their proceedings thereon, and the lands or rights of way so valued by the jury, shall vest in the Company so long as the same shall be used for the purposes of said Railroad, so soon as the valuation may be paid, or if refused, paid over to the Clerk of the County Court: *Provided,* That the right of condemnation shall not authorize the said Company to invade any dwelling house, yard, garden, or graveyard of any individual without his consent.

Authority to condemn property required by the company in case of disagreement as to value.

SEC. 18. *Be it further ordained,* That the said Company shall have the exclusive right of conveyance or transportation, of persons or goods, merchandise and produce of all kinds over said road, at such charges as may be fixed on by a majority of the Directors.

Transportation.

Profits

SEC. 19. *Be it further ordained,* That the profits of said Company, or so much thereof as the Board of Directors may deem advisable, shall, when the affairs of the Company will permit, be annually or semi-annually divided among the Stockholders in proportion to their stock.

Notice of process

SEC. 20. *Be it further ordained,* That notice of process upon the President or any of the Directors, shall be deemed and taken as due and lawful notice of service upon the Company.

Branch roads.

SEC. 21. *Be it further ordained.* That the said Company shall have power to construct branches to said road and connect with any other railroad that may be constructed, and any contract that may be entered into with any other railroad company, by the President and Directors of said Company, after the consent of a majority of the Stockholders, first obtained, shall be binding on said Company.

Authority to issue $1,000,000 in bonds.

SEC. 22. *Be it further ordained,* That it may and shall be lawful for the Fayetteville and Florence Railroad Company, to make and issue bonds to the amount not exceeding one million dollars, to be signed by the President of said Company, under the common seal of the same, in sums of one hundred dollars each, bearing interest at seven per cent., and redeemable according to the contract that may be made at the time of the sale.

Security for said bonds

SEC. 23. *Be it further ordained.* That to secure the faithful payment of said bonds, it may be lawful for the President and Directors of said Company to make and execute a mortgage or deed of trust under the common seal of said Company, wherein shall be conveyed to the person thus appointed trustee, the road, property and franchises of said Company, conditioned for the payment of the interest and final redemption of said bonds.

To be commenced within four years.

SEC. 24. *Be it further ordained.* That all the work hereby required, shall be executed with due diligence, and if it be not commenced within four years after the ratification of this ordinance, then this charter to be void.

Corporations and counties authorized to subscribe.

SEC. 25. *Be it further ordained.* That it shall be lawful for all solvent corporations to take stock in the said road, which stock, when taken, shall be represented by the

Presidents of said corporations, and in the case of a county, by the chairman of the County Court.

SEC. 26. *Be it further ordained,* That this ordinance be in force from and after its ratification, and shall be regarded as a public act, and shall be continued in force until the year nineteen hundred : *Provided,* That nothing herein contained shall be so construed at to authorize an appropriation to said road by the State, or allow said corporation banking privileges.   [*Ratified the* 12th *day of May,* 1862.]

AN ORDINANCE TO MAKE FURTHER PROVIS- [No. 39.]
ION FOR THE PUBLIC TREASURY.

1. *Be it ordained by the Delegates of the people of North Carolina, in Convention assembled, and it is hereby ordained by the authority of the same,* That the Public Treasurer is authorized to issue two millions more of Treasury notes, in sums of five dollars, ten dollars, and twenty dollars, each, in the following amounts, viz : eight hundred thousand in five dollars, seven hundred thousand in ten dollars, and five hundred thousand in twenty dollars, in accordance with the provisions of the ordinance passed February 26th, 1862, should it, in the opinion of the Governor and Treasurer, become necessary to do so, and that said notes shall be fundable, as provided for in said ordinance.

To issue $2,000,000 in Treasury notes.

2. *Be it further ordained,* That in the event of the Treasurer being unable, from any cause to issue said notes, that he be allowed to borrow any portion of said two millions from the banks or other sources.

In case of inability to issue the amount, Treasurer authorized to borrow

3. *Be it further ordained,* That the Public Treasurer be authorized to issue ten thousand dollars in denominations of five cents, and ten thousand dollars in ten cents, in addition to the amount heretofore issued by him of said denominations.

$10,000 in five and $10,000 in ten cents to be issued

4. *Be it further ordained,* That he have authority to employ some discreet person, if necessary, to be approved of by the Governor, and whose appointment shall be pub-

lished in three newspapers of this city, to sign coupon and
State bonds for the Public Treasurer.

Punishment for
forgery &c

5. *Be it further ordained,* That if any one shall falsely
forge, or knowingly pass, or offer to pass any false, forged,
or counterfeit paper purporting to be a Treasury note or
bond, or coupon of any such bond, issued under this ordinance of this State, he shall be liable to indictment in the
Superior Courts in the county in which such offence may
be committed, and on conviction therefor, shall suffer all
the pains and penalties according to the 59th section of
the 34th chapter of the Revised Code. [*Ratified the 12th
day of May,* 1862.]

[No. 10.] AN ORDINANCE DECLARING WHAT ORDI-
NANCES OF THIS CONVENTION SHALL HAVE
PERMANENT OPERATION.

Permanent
Ordinance

SECTION 1. *Be it ordained by the Delegates of the people of North Carolina in Convention assembled, and it is
hereby ordained by the authority of the same,* That following Ordinances passed by this Convention shall be of permanent operation, and be irrepealable by the General
Assembly, namely:

I. An ordinance to dissolve the union between the State
of North Carolina and the other States united with her
under the compact of Government, entitled "The Constitution of the United States."

II. "An Ordinance defining treason against the State."

III. "An Ordinance to ratify the Constitution of the
Provisional Government of the Confederate States of
America."

IV. "An Ordinance to ratify the Constitution of the
Confederate States of America."

V. "An Ordinance to amend the fourth section of the
fourth article of the Amendments to the Constitution."

VI. "An Ordinance in relation to Taxation."

VII. "An Ordinance to secure to certain officers and
soldiers the right to vote."

VIII. "An Ordinance in relation to taking to the yeas and nays in the General Assembly."

IX. "An Ordinance to amend the second section of the fourth article of the Amendments to the Constitution."

X. "An Ordinance in relation to electors of the Senate."

XI. "An Ordinance concerning the election of Governor."

XII. "An Ordinance to allow certain persons to vote for Governor in any other county than that in which they reside."

SEC. 2. *Be it further ordained,* That all other ordinances and resolutions passed by this Convention at any of its sessions, shall have the force and effect only of acts of the ordinary Legislature, and may be repealed or modified at the pleasure of the General Assembly, in the same manner and to the same extent that public statutes are liable to repeal or modification. [*Ratified the 13th day of May,* 1862.]

INDICES

TO THE

ORDINANCES AND RESOLUTIONS

OF THE

STATE CONVENTION:

FIRST AND ADJOURNED SESSIONS, 1861-'62.

23

INDEX

TO ORDINANCES AND RESOLUTIONS.

FIRST SESSION.

INDEX

TO ORDINANCES AND RESOLUTIONS.

SECOND SESSION.

INDEX

TO ORDINANCES AND RESOLUTIONS

FOURTH SESSION.

24

INDEX

TO ORDINANCES AND RESOLUTIONS.

THIRD SESSION

---

www.ingramcontent.com/pod-product-compliance
Lightning Source LLC
Chambersburg PA
CBHW020535270326
41927CB00006B/583